WALKS IN THE
SILVERDALE / ARNSIDE
AREA OF OUTSTANDING NATURAL BEAUTY

Front Cover:
On the cliff top path between White Creek
and Far Arnside
Photo: R.B.Evans

Back Cover:
Across Quicksand Pool to Warton Crag
Photo: Walt Unsworth

Cow's Mouth

WALKS IN THE

SILVERDALE/
ARNSIDE

AREA OF OUTSTANDING
NATURAL BEAUTY

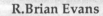

R.Brian Evans

CICERONE PRESS
MILNTHORPE, CUMBRIA

© R.B.Evans 1986
ISBN 0 902 363 78 6
First published 1986
Reprinted 1988, Revised 1990,
Reprinted 1993

TO AILEEN

To my wife Aileen for her companionship on the walks, her patience during my sketching, her research and criticism of the text, and her support at home during the many hours she saw little of me except a hunched back.

Advice to Readers

Readers are advised that whilst every effort is taken by the author to ensure the accuracy of this guidebook, changes can occur which may affect the contents. It is advisable to check locally on transport, accommodation, shops etc but even rights-of-way can be altered and, more especially overseas, paths can be eradicated by landslip, forest fires or changes of ownership.

The publisher would welcome notes of any such changes

CONTENTS

PREFACE

My parents introduced me to the Silverdale area. We would take the train to Silverdale station, walk through the woods to the village and return along the shore, catching an evening train back to Morecambe well satisfied - in season clutching brimful containers of blackberries. To a small child the woods seemed magical, a secret world where it was unwise to stray far from the path, whilst the expanse of the salt marsh was vast and lonely.

Much later my wife and I often returned to walk the paths, picnic on the shore, climb on the crags with our son, and to look at the plants and birds. Much appreciated advice and hospitality was given to us by Ted and Denise Dowbiggin at Wolf House Gallery and the Wilson family at Leighton Moss. We always had a good day in this beautiful area and it seemed a pity that little was written down about the walks, although the history of the area was well documented. It is hoped that this little book will serve a dual purpose - as an encouragement to walkers who do not yet know the area's charms, and as a reminder of many good days to those who know the region well.

Brian Evans
Preston 1986

PREFACE TO REVISED EDITION

In just four years there have been many changes in the area. The sea has gobbled up more turf, intent on turning the Silverdale cliffs into true high-tide cliffs. More waymarks, signposts and improvements to paths make easier walking.

All the routes have been checked for this amended edition and the sketch maps amended for greater clarity. Rewalking the paths confirmed my opinion that this delightful area compares favourably with many better known British beauty spots.

I hope you enjoy the walks as much as I - and my dog Beck - did. If you see a small collie with pointed ears and a penchant for sticks, I'll not be far behind. Beck is well-trained, will stop and stand still on command, and does not chase sheep. Please keep your dog under control and on a lead through farmland.

Thanks go to John Wilson who updated the bird information.

Brian Evans
Preston 1990

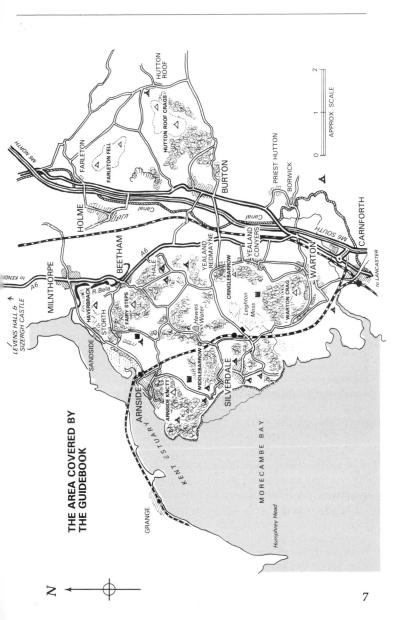

THE AREA COVERED BY
THE GUIDEBOOK

N

MORECAMBE BAY

Humphrey Head

KENT ESTUARY

GRANGE

ARNSIDE

ARNSIDE KNOTT

MIDDLEBARROW

SILVERDALE

Leighton Moss

CRINGLEBARROW

WARTON CRAG

Hawes Water

FAIRY STEPS

HAVERBRACK

STORTH

SANDSIDE

R.Bela

MILNTHORPE

to KEND

LEVENS HALL &
SIZERGH CASTLE

A6

HALE

BEETHAM

HOLME

Canal

Canal

FARLETON

FARLETON FELL

HUTTON
ROOF

HUTTON ROOF CRAGS

M6 NORTH

BURTON

YEALAND
REDMAYNE

YEALAND
CONYERS

WARTON

PRIEST HUTTON

BORWICK

CARNFORTH

M6 SOUTH

to LANCASTER

APPROX. SCALE

0   1   2

7

INTRODUCTION

The area covered by this book is compact - north to south from Milnthorpe to Carnforth it is 7 miles; west to east from Arnside Point to Hutton Roof is 8 miles. Within its confines is perhaps the most prolific concentration of high quality woodland path walking in the north of England and undoubtedly the most beautiful coastal scenery in the north-west. Much of the area lies within the Arnside/Silverdale Area of Outstanding Natural Beauty - almost the whole of the land to the west of the A6 between Warton and Milnthorpe. The equally beautiful limestone hills of Farleton Fell and Hutton Roof, to the east of the M6 were not included in the AONB, in retrospect, a regrettable omission .

Whilst the network of paths is well-walked and jealously loved by locals, it deserves wider recognition. Anyone who likes a short walk in beautiful scenery would find a visit delightful. Naturalists know the area well, for it is rich in a varied flora and fauna, especially at the several nature reserves and the RSPB Reserve at Leighton Moss.

The low wooded hills west of the M6 are easily visible to people travelling past but only hint at their attractions. Travellers have always tended to hurry through since the Lancaster to Kendal turnpike (through Burton) was established in 1752. Now six or seven minutes on the M6 and you have passed it!

Before the opening of the Carnforth-Barrow railway in 1857, travellers used the cross-bay route which has a long history of disaster. The traditional crossing was from Hest Bank to Grange, with a shorter crossing from Silverdale to Grange.

There are a surprising number of caravan parks in the area and summer visitors swell the population. It is hoped that the caravan parks will be restricted to those already there but recent plans for new holiday homes near Warton show that the AONB is not totally protected from new developments. Many of the present caravan parks nestle almost unseen amongst the trees.

Despite the caravans, the summer influx of visitors and the well-walked paths, the woods are peaceful places and away from the influence of people they provide shelter for a rich wildlife. Deer are prevalent over the whole wooded area, both native red deer and the shy, pale fallow deer, escapees from the Dallam Park herd. It is essential in order to preserve the unique qualities of the area that visitors stick to the paths, in fact progress off the path is usually so rough and impenetrable that it is unpleasant.

The AONB has a countryside management officer who keeps a watchful eye on any possible harmful developments, maintains the rights of way, carries out any necessary conservation work and aims to promote greater awareness and understanding of the area through the establishment of an informal voluntary warden service. The Countryside Management Officer can be contacted at The Old Station Building, Arnside, Tel: 0524 761034.

Walking in the area is generally on well marked paths which can be used to make circuits or linked into linear walks. Most of the routes described are short enough to be enjoyed by casual walkers or families without any need for specialist equipment or footwear. Ideal fine weather footwear are trainers or jogging shoes, which have a soft but thick, comfortable sole, thick enough to walk over stones in comfort. In wet weather muddy patches will be encountered, but boots are hardly necessary, although on Farleton Fell and Hutton Roof the terrain is more rocky and rugged, and here boots are an advantage. Note that in wet conditions, limestone can be treacherously slippery underfoot.

The walks described are short enough to fill an afternoon, or a short day, but long enough to feel that you have accomplished something. Times are based on a medium pace without taking into account any major halts. Even so, the times are generous and fast walkers could easily link two walks in a day. Remember that a fast walker sees little apart from the path at his feet, the connoisseur always takes an hour or two longer. It would be a pity to visit an area which is so rich in plant, bird and animal life and not notice much of it!

A confusing system of narrow, winding lanes network the area, and most seem to be signposted to Silverdale. There are numerous places where an odd car can be parked on the verge, but some key car parks form the main starting points for the walks.

Access

If approaching by car leave the M6 at the Carnforth junction, Exit 35. This joins the A6 at a roundabout and according to your venue, turn left for Carnforth or right to Milnthorpe. From the traffic lights in Carnforth take the Warton road, whence a choice of lanes lead to Silverdale.

Another useful approach, from the A6, is via Yealand Redmayne, whence a right turn leads past Leighton Moss to Silverdale or Arnside. From Milnthorpe a busy but very scenic road leads along the coast past Sandside to Arnside.

The Furness railway (Lancaster to Barrow) runs through the area with stations at Carnforth, Silverdale and Arnside, the two latter unmanned. At the moment there are several trains daily. Many of the walks are easily accessible from these stations, whilst the car visitor could plan a linear route to return by train.

Bus services are less frequent and times should be obtained from the Lancaster County Council Transport Enquiry Line, Lancaster 841109. Warton and Milnthorpe are easily accessible by bus and there is an infrequent service to Silverdale via Yealand and to Arnside.

Cycles can be hired from Wolf House Gallery, Silverdale.

Maps

The most useful maps of the area are the Ordnance Survey Pathfinder Series, 1:25,000. Sheet SD37/47 covers most of the Silverdale/Arnside area, but annoyingly does not include a small strip of the woodland around Cringlebarrow, nor a small section around Storth-Milnthorpe. Sheet SD57 includes the Cringlebarrow strip and most of Hutton Roof/Farleton Fell. The 1:50,000 Lancaster and Kendal sheet 97 covers the whole area but is not as detailed.

It should be possible to follow the walks from the sketch maps, which hopefully include all the important features. Many of the described walks can be inter-linked or extended. The sketch maps show various combinations. Not all the paths shown on the sketch maps are right of way or permissive paths. They are shown as an aid to navigation.

Climate

So often when the hills of the Lake District and the Pennines are shrouded with mist, the Silverdale/Arnside area enjoys good visibility and even sunshine. Annual rainfall is about 45 inches, sunshine is above average for the north-west. Mild winters mean that enjoyable walking can be done here when the weather is too violent to be attractive in other hill areas. Even strong winds are no deterrent, except on the coast, for the woodland walking is pleasantly sheltered.

Accommodation

As befits a popular holiday area, there is plenty of accommodation, bed and breakfast, holiday cottages and most popular of all - caravan and camping sites. The main sites are:

> New Barns Farm, Arnside
> Holgates Caravan Park, Middlebarrow
> Fell End Caravan Park, Hale
> Silver Ridge, Hale
> Hale More
> Beetham Caravan Park
> Hollins Farm, Far Arnside
> Hazelslack Tower Farm
> Know Hill, Silverdale
> Bottoms Farm, Silverdale
> Gibraltar Farm, Silverdale
> Cote Stones Farm, Warton
> Cragside, Hutton Roof

For small touring caravans or tents, perhaps the most idyllic of the above sites is at Gibraltar Farm, Silverdale and Cragside at Hutton Roof, although Hollins Farm and Hazelslack Tower Farm are also very attractively situated.

There is a Youth Hostel at Arnside.

Silverdale and the bay

Walking on the Shore

A unique attraction of the area is the salt marsh - a broad expanse of springy sea-washed turf patterned by narrow water-filled channels. This marsh provides a low tide walking route along the shore, and is only covered by the highest spring and autumn tides of 9m (Liverpool height). The turf does not exist all the way and there are key points where the channels come close to the shore and progress at any high tide is impossible, notably at Jack Scout and Arnside Point. At most danger points it is possible to gain cliff top paths which by-pass the difficulties.

Children find the bay environment exciting for there are rocks to scramble and little channels to jump, but take care not to wander onto the sands of the estuary as the channels can hide quicksands. Along the bay there are many warning notices which point out the danger of quicksands and the speed of incoming tides. However, at low tide it is quite safe to walk on the sands close to the shore edge, although it can be messy underfoot in places.

Sheep graze on the marsh, so dogs need to be kept under control. Erosion in recent years has drastically cut the amount of grazing, as the Kent channel has swung closer to the Silverdale shore.

An additional attraction of walking on the shore is the birdlife. The marsh is part of the RSPB reserve and is a nationally important site, a feeding and roosting area for thousands of waders, wildfowl and gulls. At high tide Jenny Brown's Point is a good vantage point to watch waders. The coastal path is also a popular bird watching vantage point - at either end of Silverdale bay. Also recommended is the Kent Estuary. It is worth a special visit to the coast in winter to see the vast flocks of dunlin, knot, oystercatcher and redshank which gather on the edge of the tide.

Shelduck, a colourful bird which finds its food in the estuary mud, is often seen in large numbers. Greylag geese are sometimes common in winter.

The shore is a place to visit at all seasons and state of tides.

Walking in the Woods

The wonderful woodland walking contrasts nicely with that of the open bay. Several of the walks combine a bit of both. A criticism so often levelled at forest walking is that the trees are all the same, the views restricted, the paths dull. The natural woodland walking in this area is completely different: the trees are constantly changing - there are huge spreading yews, or wand-like hazels, grand oak and beech, evergreen larch and pine, ash and hornbeam.

The paths are rarely dull, for they run over a thin soiled limestone, where the craggy structure is constantly poking through. There are limestone pavements, where many of the crevices sprout prickly hawthorns, delightful in blossom time. Craglets, often clothed in rich

The woodland carpet - wood anemones burst through Dog's Mercury

mosses and trees, are either companions to the path or barriers to be crossed. Where the woodland thins, there are pleasant clearings fringed by brambles which can be profitably visited in season.

Views are certainly restricted at times, especially in the height of summer greenery, but the paths are rarely boring, for they are not too wide and often weave an intricate course amongst the craglets. Suddenly a clearing may reveal a glimpse of silvery Morecambe Bay or the surrounding hills. Walking off the paths is unpleasantly rough and ill-advised.

The woods support a prolific but shy wildlife. Deer can often be seen, but they prefer undisturbed surroundings and usually keep away from the popular paths. Badger setts can sometimes be seen, but you will only see these shy nocturnal creatures if you are very lucky around twilight.

Until around 1914 most of the woodland in this area was managed on the coppice-with-standards system, in which the standards, often oak, were allowed to grow normally, whilst the surrounding underwood, usually of hazel or ash, was cut down. The felled trees produced a growth of straight, slender wood which was then harvested for poles or brushwood. Coppice or copse derives from the French word *couper* to cut. During the First World War many of the standards were cut down and coppicing went into decline. The wood was often used for the flourishing bobbin industry of South Westmorland and for charcoal manufacture.

The woodland walking is delightful all year round as every season holds a special charm. Perhaps most rewarding is late spring to early summer, when the trees are bursting to life with delicate fresh green leaves, and flowers carpet the floor of the wood in a spray of colour - whether it is the purple of the violets, the white wood anemones, yellow primroses or daffodils, or the pink of herb robert. Almost all year round the woodland carpet is dog's mercury. Its early shoots accompany the snowdrop, its star patterned leaves hide the ground and provide a backdrop for the more colourful flowers the rest of the year.

High summer is predominantly green - and sometimes too lush for comfortable walking where the paths are slender. Here the trails take on a jungle character where you follow too closely at your peril or you may suffer the whiplash of a punitive branch. However most of the popular walks are on paths which are broad enough to traverse

In Potts Wood, Warton Crag

comfortably even at the zenith of vegetation growth.

October is another highpoint of the year when the autumnal blaze of colours are at their best. This is the time to seek out the stately beeches in Eaves Wood, although caution is necessary on the leaf-covered paths where slippery limestone lurks unseen. When winds blow too strongly for comfort on the shore, the woods can be pleasantly sheltered.

Autumn is particularly good for fungi. Especially interesting are the tiny species - elf cups, fairy clubs, earth stars, bird's nest fungi and many more.

Winter is not to be despised for the delicate tracery of stripped branches can be very attractive. There is a surprising amount of greenery still around - the moss which covers both rock and tree trunk, ivy is particularly abundant and much more obvious in winter. It wreaths around trunks, creeps over boulders and walls and sometimes seems to be devouring the long, low crags, aided by the green velvet-like moss. Lattice patterns of branches capture sunlight like a stained glass window. Wands and branches weave in the wind as though conducting the orchestra as the trees rustle and creak in a never ending tune-up before the great woodland symphony begins.

Almost all the paths described are rights of way. There are numerous other woodland paths mainly on the Leighton Hall Estate and Dallam Tower Estate where walkers are not welcome. Sometimes what appears to be a popular footpath is merely a short path to a netted pheasant rearing enclosure. Some of these are close to the rights of way and birds can often be seen - as can their carcasses when a fox has been active.

Dog Rose

Geology

All the hills in the area are formed of Carboniferous limestone which was uplifted at the end of the Carboniferous period, about 350 million years ago, to its present block and basin structure, although considerable erosion has taken place since then. The blocks of limestone have a gentle dip usually to the south or south-east as at Farleton, but north-east at Warton Crag, due to the effects of faulting.

The north-south valleys are fault controlled and the lines of several north-south faults can be traced throughout the area, particularly the Trough. Where it runs through Trowbarrow Quarry it is easy to see how rock movement has caused the rock strata to become almost vertical, or even reversed.

Between the blocks of limestone are basins which are floored with sediments or alluvium, which gives good farm land where well drained - or forms the marshy area such as Leighton Moss and Haweswater. Around Haweswater is found diatomite, which is composed of the siliceous fossil remains of microscopic organisms. It is a valuable commodity, used for its insulation properties and was worked commercially at Kentmere in the Lake District. Hollows are typical of limestone scenery. Small ones, often with a water sink at the base are called dolines. A good example is at Deepdale but well hidden in woods. Haweswater lies on several merged dolines. The larger basins are called *poljes* after huge examples in Yugoslavia where they often fill to become lakes in wet weather or winter. Hale Moss is a good example here. The *poljes* occur in chains and would have been lakes in glacial times.

A considerable thickness of ice covered the area during the last Ice Age and as this melted Morecambe Bay covered a much larger area than it does now. One theory is that ice in the Irish Sea made Morecambe Bay into a gigantic lake. The present day hollows were all submerged at that time and it is easy to visualize the Arnside and Silverdale hills as islands. The edges of the hollows were sometimes lined by small sea cliffs - like the one close to the road at the edge of Hale Moss. These cliffs are riddled with small tubular water-worn passages. There is evidence of several sea levels along the Silverdale coast, and an almost perfect circular phreatic tube cave worn by water pressure action.

The deep runnels on the surface of the tilted limestone pavements are especially pronounced on Farleton Fell and Hutton Roof Crags, where the rounded *rundkarren* are amongst the best examples in Britain. These were formed when the rocks were covered by a layer of vegetation and water draining away wore the limestone into its present attractive patterns. Sharp edged *rinnenkarren* were formed where the rocks were open to the weather. Hutton Roof and Farleton Fell lay directly in line with the advancing Morecambe Bay ice. During the last Ice Age many limestone blocks were moved and deposited on other limestone beds. There are many examples of these perched blocks in the vicinity, one specially noted on Walk No.18.

Just south of the main limestone beds are conical reef knolls, small grassy hills well seen around Carnforth. Reef is a misnomer for they are really lime-mud banks bound by crinoids and corals. South again are beds of red sandstone, which at one time covered the limestone before it eroded away. An interesting feature which developed at this time was due to water seeping through the sandstone and becoming impregnated with minerals which were deposited in the limestone caves below. This is an explanation of the presence of copper and haematite which were mined in several parts of the area, especially at Crag Foot, where layers of brecciated sandstone filled the phreatic passages.

Copper ore was mined in Elizabethan times near Jenny Brown's Point and a little later near Storth. Copper was mined at Crag Foot between 1800 and 1830 by Cornish miners. The ore was smelted at Jenny Brown's Point, the smelt mill built at the end of the 18th century. The engines were transported from North Wales. Copper was scarce at this time and highly prized. Leighton furnace was built in 1713 and operated until the 1800's.

The Higher and Lower Warton Mines at Crag Foot enjoyed a further lease of life between 1836 and 1840 when the haematite ore was mined for reddle, a very powerful red dye used in the manufacture of paint and prized for the dye used for colouring doorway threshold stones. The ore was floated, dried, crushed and screened, then roasted to give different colours.

On a personal note my son and a friend, both experienced mine explorers, enjoyed a trip in the Crag Foot mines to emerge plastered in sticky red mud which clung to their clothes for months despite washing. Months later there were still traces of red along the road where they had walked.

Archaeologically interesting is Dog Holes, above Crag Foot on

Warton Crag, though there is no public access. At the foot of a small shaft are several galleries which have yielded a rich collection of remains, the earliest dated from Late Pleistocene times. Beaker ware, flints and human remains from Neolithic times, Bronze Age enamelled bronzework and pans, and Roman pottery have been recovered. It seems that the cave was used a long, long time for human habitation. Other archaeological remains have been found at another Dog Holes, on Haverbrack, but not in the same quantity as at Warton.

Rock Climbing

The limestone scars are well used by rock climbers, both those living locally and those driven away from the Lake District in their search for dry rock. There are many small outcrops, some of which form valuable gymnasiums for dedicated climbers to train unroped on problem climbs of great difficulty. This brief résumé of the climbing in the area is intended to enlighten non-rock climbers who are using this book and promote some understanding.

Warton Upper Crag

On the edge of **Warton village** there is a car park in a small quarry, where climbers can often be seen. The rock is steep and somewhat shattered but there are numerous problem climbs on the vegetated cliffs. It is traditional to do a few climbs here, then walk up to other crags. On a terrace about half-way up the hill and almost directly above the Main Quarry is another little horizontal scar - the **Pinnacle Crag,** named after a small pinnacle at its foot. Almost hidden by trees, this crag is solid and seamed with cracks and grooves which provide many medium standard climbs. After playing here for a while we move on to the short open scar which crowns the top of the hill. This is **Warton Upper Crag** and is the most popular of the rocks for climbers of medium standard. Most limestone is very steep and offers climbing for experts only. Here the rock is friendly as it lies back a little, is full of huge holds and is solidly attached.

The **Main Quarry** is a complete contrast. The climbs here are over 200 feet long on loose rock in very serious situations. Since the first climb was made in 1970 it has been networked with routes, the best of which are very impressive. It is worth walking into the far end of the quarry to see just what climbers climb, for the most impressive routes take a series of fearsome grooves and overhangs. Quarry climbing is a relatively recent development which caused concern amongst quarry owners. An Act of Parliament should have done much to clear up any problems of liability in case of accidents and should help to limit access problems. It is a crying shame that in these days of increased leisure activities quarries are not recognized for what they are - valuable assets as a sporting facility for young people. Some councils spend thousands of pounds on creating climbing walls and bar access to natural facilities!

The only other climbing area of more than local interest is at **Trowbarrow Quarry,** much more popular than Warton Main as the rock is very sound in places. There are several clean slabs, one of which is seamed with cracks and covered with fossils which provide useful rugosities. Trowbarrow is another quarry where access has created problems in the past. It is hoped that these problems are now sorted out and that climbing will be tolerated - at least until requarrying starts if ever!

Another interesting climbing cliff lies on the coast at **Jack Scout Cove.** (Note the local name is Cow's Mouth.) Here is the nearest thing Lancashire possesses to a genuine sea cliff, indeed at high tide water washes the base of the crags and has resulted in some rock falls. The climbs here are steep and enter a zone of vegetation above the clean rocks.

Other training crags are at **Woodwell** and **Fairy Steps. Farleton Crag** is a steep band of cliffs hidden amongst the trees and barely visible from the motorway although the upper crag's steep nose is well visible. **Hutton Roof Crags** offer attractive little climbs especially on **The Rakes,** an intriguingly complex area akin to Indian country. This is an ideal spot to take youngsters.

All these crags are mentioned in the text, as walks go past or near them.

The climbs are all named and documented in detail in *Rock Climbs in Lancashire and the North West* (Cicerone Press). The party which makes the first ascent has the dubious honour of naming the climb, and the names make fascinating reading, from the mundane 'Original Route' to descriptive 'White Fright' (very loose!) to the exotic 'Essence of Giraffe' (you need to stick your neck out to lead this one). Other interesting names are 'Limestone Rain,' 'Plastic Iceberg,' 'The Onedin Line' (a traverse at Jack Scout Cove), 'The Shriek of Baghdad.' They're an inventive lot, these climbers!

The Rakes, Hutton Roof Crags

SHORT WALKS

A specially attractive feature of the area is the wealth of short walks of high quality, which are ideal for a family who want a stroll or a picnic. Listed below are some of the best parking spots from which a stroll is especially rewarding. These are all visited by the described walks and are marked on the accompanying sketch maps.

THE SHORE
Silverdale Shore

There is a car park on the shore, reached down Shore Road from the Post Office. A justly popular centre for short walks in both directions along the sea-washed turf. Note that the highest spring and autumn tides cover the turf and on no account stray on the estuary sands which can be dangerous. Heed the warning notices. See Walks No.1 and 2.

Silverdale Cove

At the north end of Silverdale village, Cove Road gives access to the shore, with space for car parking through the gate. This is similar to the above for walks along the greensward at the base of the limestone cliffs. There are two small but interesting caves, irresistible to the adventurous child. See Walk No.2.

Jenny Brown's Point and Jack Scout

A narrow lane leads from Gibraltar, a little south of Silverdale village, to reach the shore edge at Jenny Brown's Point. Cars must not be driven past the sign and care must be taken with the limited parking space, not to block access. The shore is delightful - easy walking to the south towards the old copper smelt mill chimney at Brown's Cottages, or more scrambly along the rocks past the old jetty towards Silverdale village. Note that every high tide sweeps right up to the cliffs here.

From the same access point a few yards back up the lane there is access to the National Trust headland of Jack Scout, one of the most beautiful little places in the whole area, with widespread views across the bay, a network of little footpaths which run between dense patches of scrub and bushes, and the Giant's Seat - a large stone seat in a commanding position. There are two other access points to the National Trust land, from higher up the lane. See Walk No.1.

Arnside

At the end of the promenade is a limited space for car parking. A path leads along the edge of the shore for as far as you care to go - to the bay of New Barns or White Creek. The sands are not particularly good for walking as several deep channels come close to the shore. A warning hooter is sounded at the approach of the tide which can roll in at an amazing speed. It is worth a special visit just to witness this, especially at the highest tides when you may be fortunate enough to see the Arnside Bore. This is a much smaller version of the Severn Bore and its height rarely exceeds a couple of feet. Canoeists sometimes await the arrival of the bore and attempt to ride it as the surge sweeps up the narrowing estuary to culminate in an exciting shoot through the turbulent water under the viaduct arches. Here the tide builds up against the piers to create a considerable rapid through the arches and a fearsome set of eddies on the upstream side. Needless to say this is only attempted by the very experienced canoeists who are confident and expert at handling their craft in rough water. See Walk No.11.

THE WOODS AND HILLS

Arnside Knott

A justly popular spot on a fine day. Drive up the hill from the promenade, follow signs to 'The Knott' and the road ends at a large car park set amongst trees just below the final slopes of the Knott. The views are good here, even better from the View Indicator at the top of the first steep rise of the Knott. Paths radiate from the car park and all are attractive. A superb place for a picnic on a warm summer day and a beautiful spot from which to observe sunset over the bay. Great for the children to play amongst the maze of small trees. See Walk No.12.

Fairy Steps

Park near the top of the Beetham-Storth road and follow a gently rising path into the woods to the Fairy Steps - a narrow cleft which affords a scrambly way through the steep limestone crag. See Walks No.7, 14 and 15.

Eaves Wood

From the National Trust car park at the edge of Eaves Wood, a nature trail can be followed, or shorter walks made. Don't miss going to the

Pepper Pot on the edge of Cringlebarrow - if you can find it! See Walk No.5.

Warton Crag Nature Reserve

Park in the small quarry just up the steep lane from the Black Bull, or if full, there are other vergeside parking spots a little further along the lane. Warton Crag is one of the best places in the whole area for short walks, several trails leading from the quarry onto the terraced flanks of the fell. There is a short nature trail and abundant blackberries in season. Signs at path entry points show the permissive paths. See Walk No.4.

Woodwell

A lane gives access to Woodwell from Lindeth Road which links Silverdale village to Gibraltar. There is a small car park near a pool fed by well waters. Paths run along the base and top of the crag and also a very pleasant path leads through woods to Silverdale village. See Walks No.1 and 3.

Burton Well

From Bottoms Lane at Silverdale Green a short circuit can be made into the very pleasant woods, past the clearing where Burton Well emerges and back to Bottoms Lane - or continue to the golf course and the station.

Hutton Roof Crags

Park on the roadside near the highest point of the lane between Farleton and Hutton Roof fells. A stile gives access to Hutton Roof Crags and its maze of paths amongst the limestone. See Walk No.19.

Hutton Roof village

Parking is very limited but it is an excellent starting point for short walks amongst the striking rock scenery and velvet turf of The Rakes. See Walks No.20 and 21.

The Lancaster-Kendal canal

The old towpath is ideal for short walks or a picnic, and access is readily available at numerous points - perhaps best between Burton and Holme where the canal swings away from the motorway for a while and the drone of traffic is not a distraction. The stretch between Borwick and Capernwray is also recommended. See Walks No.22 and 23.

HISTORIC BUILDINGS IN THE AREA

There are several buildings of historic interest in the area, some of which are open to the public at certain times. Most are visited on the walks, where a more detailed description is given in the text.

Heron Corn Mill and Museum of Paper-Making (See Walk No.14)
One of the best surviving examples of a water-driven corn mill. Follow signs from Beetham to the car park by the river. Open to the public April to September, Tuesday to Sunday 11.00am.-5.00pm. Café and picnic area.

Leighton Hall (See Walks No.3 and 8)
Open May to September, Wednesday, Sundays and Bank Holidays. 2.30pm.-6.00pm. Approach by the Coach Road from Warton. The Hall has a white Gothic facade almost like a medieval fort. Free-flying eagles and other birds of prey.

Levens Hall (See Walk No.24)
Open Easter to end of September. House open Tuesdays, Wednesdays, Thursdays and Sundays 2.00pm.-5.00pm. Gardens open daily. The 16th century Levens Hall is famous for its topiary gardens planned in 1689. The largest Elizabethan house in Cumbria, incorporating a massive 14th century pele tower. Worth visiting to see the fine carved panelling, chimney-pieces and coats-of-arms. A further attraction is the Steam Collection - table engines, beam engines and hot-air engines. Well worth a visit.

Sizergh Castle
Open April to end of September on Sundays, Wednesdays and Thursdays. Just west of the A6 a mile or so north of Levens Hall. Follow sign from A6. The castle is mainly Elizabethan incorporating a mid-14th century pele tower. Home of the Strickland family. Noted for its richly carved interior panelling and particularly attractive gardens. Owned by the National Trust.

Borwick Hall (See Walk No.23)
Open to the public only on special Open Days. Now a residential centre owned by the Lancashire Youth Clubs' Association. Borwick Hall is a splendid Elizabethan building with fine gardens. Renowned for its ghost - the White Lady. For information concerning Open Days write to The Warden, Borwick Hall Residential Centre, Borwick, Nr. Carnforth, Lancs. LA6 1JU.

The Pele Towers (See Walks No.2, 6, 7, 13 and 15)
All of the pele towers in the area are in a dangerous condition and are not open to the public. Nevertheless much of interest can be seen from the exterior.

The towers were built around the 15th century, often on the site of earlier buildings, as a defensive ring around Morecambe Bay, in order to safeguard the local inhabitants and their animals from marauding Scots. The biggest was **Arnside Tower** with others at **Hazelslack, Beetham, Dallam, Borwick** and **Wraysholme.** Towers at **Sizergh** and **Levens** were later incorporated into larger buildings (which are open to the public).

CHURCHES
Of the churches in the area the most interesting are at **Warton, Beetham** and **Heversham.**

Warton Church is renowned for its associations with the Washington family, and the worn flagstone bearing the stars and stripes of the family arms can be seen inside the church. It was moved to there from the tower to prevent further weathering.

Beetham Church is a particularly lovely old building, approached by a trellis-covered path complete with roses.

Heversham Church is one of the oldest churches in Westmorland with such a long and interesting history that a local historian, Roger Bingham, produced a book on the subject - *The Church at Heversham*. There is a commanding view from the tower across the Kent Estuary.

Heversham Church

THE WALKS

Silverdale/Arnside
Area

SOUTH ALONG THE SHORE FROM SILVERDALE Walk 1

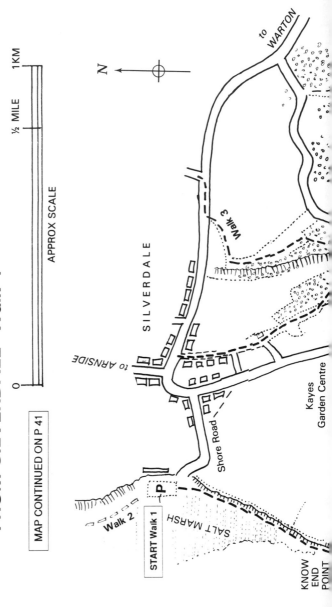

MAP CONTINUED ON P 41

APPROX SCALE

0   ½ MILE   1KM

N

SILVERDALE

to ARNSIDE

to WARTON

Kayes Garden Centre

Shore Road

SALT MARSH

START Walk 1

Walk 2

Walk 3

P

KNOW END POINT

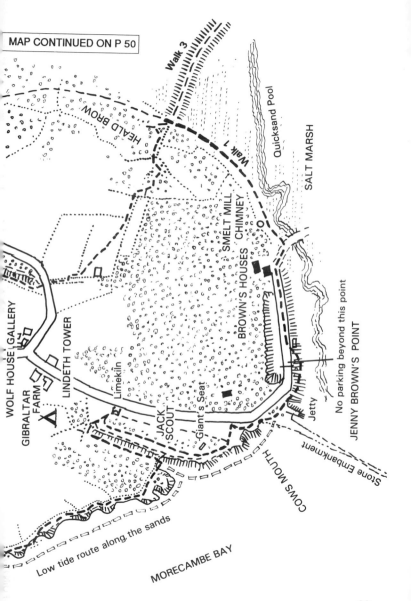

MAP CONTINUED ON P 50

Walk 3

HEALD BROW

Walk 1

Quicksand Pool

SALT MARSH

SMELT MILL CHIMNEY

BROWN'S HOUSES

WOLF HOUSE GALLERY

GIBRALTAR FARM

LINDETH TOWER

Limekiln

JACK SCOUT

Giant's Seat

No parking beyond this point

Jetty

JENNY BROWN'S POINT

Stone Embankment

COWS MOUTH

Low tide route along the sands

MORECAMBE BAY

29

1. South along the shore from Silverdale
Return over Heald Brow and Woodwell
3½ miles
2-2½ hours (rough and rocky in parts)

A delightful circuit, one of the best in the area. At low tide the sands can be followed entirely. At high tide the section between Know End Point and Jenny Brown's Point is impassable along the shore. Ideally you should do the walk twice - once along the sands and once along the cliff top paths, for each has its attractions. Perhaps the best is a combination of the two as described. Note that tides over 9 metres (Liverpool height) come over the salt marsh.

Since erosion of the sea level turf, this walk has become more difficult at high tide, and involves a scramble onto a narrow cliff top path. Suitable footwear is essential.

Start at the shore car park at the end of Shore Road.

Walk south along the turf at the foot of a low line of gorse-topped crags. Keep close to the cliffs to avoid the numerous small channels on the marsh. At Know End Point pass an RSPB notice which warns of fast incoming tides.

You may see shelduck feeding on the sands, although without binoculars it is difficult to see the distinctive tan flash on their breast. Views across the bay are wide - from the clustered tiered houses of Grange on the right, past the low wooded hump of Humphrey Head to the distant chimneys of Barrow. On the left side of the bay are the squat towers of Heysham Power Station. Dominating everything is

The cliff top approaching Cow's Mouth

the expanse of glistening sand and water channels of the bay.

The grass ends - at the time of writing - at Know End Point where at high tide recourse must be made to the cliff top. A rock scramble of 20 feet or so onto the cliff edge reveals a tiny crumbly path which can be followed with care. This is safer than traversing the slimy rocks at sea level. At low tide there is no problem as the cliff top path can be gained where it improves above 200 yards further, but if the sands are followed all the way you will certainly get wet feet and messy footwear. The high tide route descends into the third small pebbly cove and regains the cliff top at its end. The airy path becomes easier and broader. Pass a craggy inlet and go over a headland into the deeper inlet of Cow's Mouth. I remember this when turf as smooth as a bowling green abutted the crags. Now it is a genuine sea cliff.

Cow's Mouth from the sands

*Walk No 1 goes south along the shore from Silverdale. This photograph,
looking north along the cliffs towards Know End Point, shows the extent
of the sea-washed turf in 1985.*

*Overleaf shows the same place in 1990. All the turf has gone and at
high tide recourse must be made to the narrow path along the cliff top.*

An impressive crag lines the east side of the cove, one of the north-south faults so prevalent in the area. It is a popular place for rock climbing although the base of the crag is covered at high tide and the rock is rather shattered. Note the red triangular scar above a small cave in the centre of the crag, where a large rock detached itself in 1983. The cave is on a mineral vein and is an old mine trial.

At all but high tide the walk along the sands can be continued, but note the incoming tide sweeps in rapidly! Just round the corner from the cliffs a break gives access to a stile in the National Trust land of Jack Scout. At high tide water bars the way at Cow's Mouth and the following route must be taken, although the first part is not a right of way and is only permissible by the generosity of the farmer.

From the back of Cow's Mouth take a path along the foot of a shallow wooded dell of great charm and where the crags on the right fizzle out take a slight path right to a square sheep hole in the wall. This is just before reaching the main camping field of Gibraltar Farm, one of the nicest campsites in the area. Creep through the hole, and emerge onto the bushy heath of Jack Scout. This National Trust land is an idyllic area of little paths and clearings amidst clusters of gorse and small trees.

The path straight ahead soon opens into a clearing where a restored limekiln stands. It is interesting to see how the top of the kiln was lined with sandstone to prevent the kiln itself burning away! Do not go directly down the field from the kiln, but bear right over a slight rise to join another track, turn left along this and soon reach the top edge of Cow's Mouth above trees. Further left, almost at the highest point is the Giant's Seat, a large slab of limestone with a walled back, in a commanding position. The prospect is so good that the seat is irresistible. It is a good spot to watch the tide racing in, far more reassuring than from the foot of the cliffs! In winter you will see huge flocks of dunlin and knott which congregate in very tight groups and feed on the sand as the tide comes in.

Drop toward the shore to a path close to the fence and pass two stiles which give access to the sands. At a little dip another stile can be crossed to the shore if you like scrambling across the rocks or sticky walking on the sands. An easier route lies up the path in the dip

Know Point and the cliff top path, 1990 (Walk 1.)

Limekiln, Jack Scout
before renovation in 1986

towards the road. Ignore the gate onto the road and a second one - descend right to stones at the head of the breakwater and the old jetty at Jenny Brown's Point. Continue over rock slabs to reach the lane at a seat.

The ruined stone jetty of Jenny Brown's Point was built to facilitate the construction of the copper smelt mill. It is difficult to imagine ships tying up against it, but at the time, the late 18th century, the channel must have been deep enough.

From the same point there is a ruined stone embankment which runs a considerable distance into the bay. This is a relic of an over ambitious land reclamation scheme of 1873. It was intended to reclaim the marshes between Jenny Brown's Point and Hest Bank, but the company ran out of funds and the scheme was abandoned. Until 1977 the embankment lay buried beneath the sand, when changes in the channel revealed it. Now it is being buried again.

The road comes close on the left, a popular access point for motorists but with very limited parking space. Behind is a long quarry, where stone was obtained for the breakwater. Now the farmer uses it to house sheep and it must contain one of the world's longest feeding troughs! Erosion of recent years has considerably reduced the amount of grazing on the salt marsh. It's not much consolation to know that the channel swings backwards and forwards

Giant's Seat

between the Grange and Silverdale sides of the estuary about every 75 years.

Round the corner past Brown's Cottages is the prominent chimney - all that remains of the copper smelting mill. Copper was mined on the hill close by in Elizabethan times and until much later across the marsh at Crag Foot on the flanks of Warton Crag. See notes on p.18. The chimney at Crag Foot was part of a pumping station which drained the flat land around Leighton Moss.

Another type of erosion is evident as we continue along the turf - there are square patches where the turf has been rolled up, destined for someone's lawn!

Cross a stile and reach an embankment, the relic of the Crag Foot scheme. Here we leave the coast and take a path left, signed 'Woodwell.' Go through a gate and take a path diagonally right uphill. After a short way it passes under a tree. Do not take this route but go diagonally left on a smooth green path above the gorse. This soon becomes more obvious and leads to a fence. Go up close to the fence to a slit stile. Pass through a patch of dense trees followed by scrub to the top of Heald Brow. Re-enter woods (red arrows pointing other way). At a junction bear up right to fence and stile left. Go ahead at side of wall, pass a gap in another wall and go diagonally right past a new farm building to a gate. Join a narrow track on the left to reach the road 50 yards ahead. (Wolf House Gallery lies a few minutes left:

36   *The Smelt Mill Chimney and Quicksand Pool*

The embankment at Jenny Brown's Point in 1986

craft centre, art gallery and café.)

Cross the road and descend a path which runs below the long line of overgrown crags. Ivy covers the boulders at its foot and trees sprout from the most unlikely crevices. A square pool is reached, whose waters are fuelled by a well at the foot of the crags. This is Woodwell, once an important watering spot for drovers' cattle, now a popular picnic spot. There is an adjacent car park and from it, by a seat, a path runs into the wood. The floor of the wood is carpeted with anemones and wood garlic. Pass through a gap in a wall and turn right along a path to the first houses of Silverdale village. Past a cottage keep right on a path between the houses and the woods. Go through a walled snicket, pass a private lane, to reach the main road. Turn left along this and down Shore Road to the car park.

2. North along the shore from Silverdale
Return over Heathwaite and Arnside Tower
5³/₄ miles
2³/₄-3¹/₄ hours

A highly recommended circuit from Silverdale, with a good variety of walking and scenery. The walk is described from the Silverdale shore car park at the end of Shore Road, but could be done equally well from the smaller car park at the Cove, reached from Cove Road.

Start: The car park lies at the edge of a broad expanse of salt marsh and is a very popular spot. On the edge of the car park is a spring - Bard Well - which was covered when the car park was first built but after water forced a way through the rubble it is now edged by stones.

Walk north along the turf at the foot of small limestone cliffs. If there have been high tides or rain, several small channels may need to be leapt or avoided by detours before reaching Silverdale Cove. These squiggly, narrow, water-filled hollows are a feature of the salt marsh and form an attractive pattern when viewed from the cliff top. Fresh water percolates from below and forms a line of springs at the foot of the cliffs, whilst the channels and pools are topped-up at high tides. In a long dry spell they can dry out. Close to the cliffs the channels are less defined and this makes the easiest walking. Again, they are less defined close to the estuary edge but here several deep, muddy inlets create obstacles.

On the right just as the Cove is reached, lies the deep red gash of Red Rake, once tunnelled by miners in search of copper and haematite. Now the entrance is collapsed, but the site is interesting to geologists. On the opposite side of the Cove is a black circular hole in the cliffs, a conspicuous landmark which invites a scramble into its interior. It is a phreatic cave, worn by water pressure when the water level was higher and possibly enlarged by man.

The most interesting of the Silverdale caves lies about 100 yards further along the cliffs. Its entrance is a low porch, just about head high and in wet weather guarded by a shallow pool. Inside, the roof is higher and the cave can be explored with a torch. A tall, narrow rift leads on, past a small rock scramble to end in a small chamber. It is

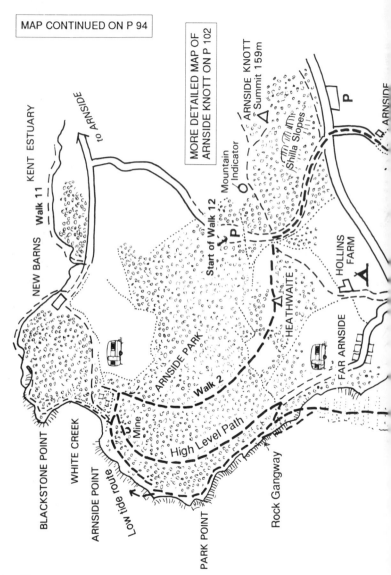

MAP CONTINUED ON P 94

MORE DETAILED MAP OF ARNSIDE KNOTT ON P 102

ARNSIDE KNOTT Summit 159m

ARNSIDE

P

Shilla Slopes

Mountain Indicator

P

Start of Walk 12

HOLLINS FARM

HEATHWAITE

KENT ESTUARY

to ARNSIDE

NEW BARNS Walk 11

ARNSIDE PARK

Walk 2

FAR ARNSIDE

BLACKSTONE POINT

WHITE CREEK

ARNSIDE POINT

Low tide route

Mine

High Level Path

PARK POINT

Rock Gangway

40

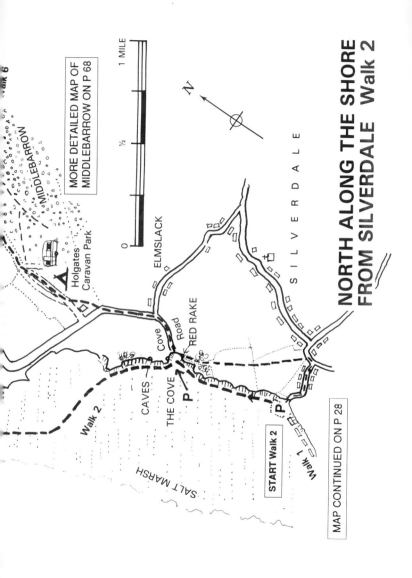

MORE DETAILED MAP OF
MIDDLEBARROW ON P 68

1 MILE

ELMSLACK

MIDDLEBARROW

Holgates
Caravan Park

Cove Road

RED RAKE

CAVES

THE COVE

P

SALT MARSH

Walk 2

START Walk 2

Walk 1

P

S I L V E R D A L E

MAP CONTINUED ON P 28

NORTH ALONG THE SHORE
FROM SILVERDALE Walk 2

quite safe and invariably the high point of the walk for impression-able youngsters. Shine up a shaft which rises almost to the crag top. Look at the tiny stalactites on the roof and walls; the rich red of the iron-stained rock walls; the water-worn scallops in the rift. It is a little insight into the attractions of caving.

Continue along the turf at the foot of the cliffs. There is a notice, one of several along the bay, warning of quicksands and fast rising tides. The quicksands are in the estuary and at all but the highest tides (over 9 metres) walking on the salt marsh turf is quite safe. Once the high tides reach the level of the turf it sweeps in with great speed. It is worth making a special note of the year's highest spring and autumn tides just to see how far the water comes at such times.

The vegetated cliffs are a veritable vertical rockery, pink and grey shattered limestone sprouts a variety of plants including

Silverdale Cove

wild strawberries, stonecrop, coltsfoot, thrift and celandine - and a few wallflowers, probably escapees from nearby gardens.

Pass a small cave at the foot of the rocks and just before the next cove negotiate a particularly muddy depression, fortunately furnished with stepping-stones. At this cove, where the road can be seen on the

right, it makes a change to leave the cliff foot and cross the turf to its edge where the estuary erosion of recent years can be seen. The Kent Channel is never constant and shifts its course from year to year. Over a ten-year period the channel has moved from the Grange side of the bay towards the Silverdale side, with consequent erosion of the turf. Silverdale marsh is reasonably protected from the worst erosion as the channel is forced out by Park Point, but at the southern end of the marsh towards Jenny Brown's Point (see Walk No.1), the erosion has been devastating.

Continue north along the flat grass and sandy depressions towards the wooded point which bounds the end of the marsh. Keep fairly well out on the grass as there are many maze-like channels closer to the shore. Even so, several channels need to be leapt or avoided.

Note the caravan site which nestles amongst the trees and aim for a pebble beach at its far end. Just past this a path leads into the woods and continues just above low broken cliffs. In season it is bordered by myriads of wild daffodils and violets. A more exciting way to the cliff top path is to continue on the shore well past the pebble beach. In a little rocky cove a slanting rock shelf provides a smooth but airy way

Red Rake

Sheep graze on the salt marsh - Arnside Knott behind

to join the upper path.

The small path from the pebble beach soon joins the broader track from the caravan site and we are faced with a choice.

CLIFF TOP ROUTE: Follow the path left. This keeps close to the cliff edge and is narrow and exposed in places, although its situation makes it perhaps the most scenic coastal path in the north-west as it twists above rocky coves on a narrow grassy ribbon on the edge of the dense woods. It is described in reverse on Walk No.11 from Arnside. (At a headland another alternative is offered by a gangway path down to the sands at low water.) At the cove of White Creek turn right at a wall into the woods. Pass the junction of the high level path on the right.

HIGH LEVEL PATH: Turn right through a gate and rise to another path junction in 50 yards. Go left along this pleasant broad path through the woods, parallel to and at a higher level from the cliff top path. Views over the bay are restricted to tantalising glimpses through the trees. On the right pass the entrance to White Creek mine, a small trial in the search for haematite. Soon the path drops to join the cliff top path at a wall.

Turn right at a T-junction a few yards further (left leads to White Creek Caravan Site). The forest lane soon swings left into private woods - we keep straight on steeply up the hill amongst the trees of Arnside Park. This is not a right of way, but is a very well used path. All side tracks into the woods are defended by 'Private' signs, so do not stray!

At last the path levels and a gate is reached and soon a clearing with widespread views over the bay. We are now on the hill crest and the views are more open, a delightful place. Keep on the main path as it rises over the top of Heathwaite. Arnside Knott can be seen poking above the trees ahead and our path drops to its shoulder where there is a major path junction. Just through the gate turn right on a bridle track, signed Arnside Tower, which gradually descends around the steep base of the Knott. On the left are the steep shattered rock screes of the Shilla slopes formed by glacial action and weathering. Shilla is a local word for scree. The slopes are of particular interest to geologists and are easily damaged. A lot of stabilising work has been done and people are asked to keep away.

Our path descends to the road, which we cross and continue on the farm lane towards the prominent ruin of Arnside Tower. This is the largest of the pele towers in the area and was built in the 15th century

as a defence against marauding Scots, although an earlier tower was built on the same site in 1375. Its position on a low saddle between Arnside Knott and Middlebarrow makes it a distinctive landmark, whilst in times of danger signals could be seen from other nearby towers and across the bay.

Keep to the right of the farmhouse and pass the stark ruin which is in a dangerous condition and should not be entered. During a violent storm in 1884 a corner of the tower collapsed. Do not go through the stile beyond the tower, but take the gate immediately before the stile on the right, which opens onto a green lane pleasantly bordered by a hedgerow rich in flowers. At one point, there is a whole bank of green helebore, the peculiar green flowered plant rare elsewhere but

The gangway up the cliffs

so common in the Arnside area. Through a gate enter the edge of a huge caravan site, and follow the upper tarmac lane to the site entrance, but just before the buildings keep left on a path which cuts the corner to the road. Turn left along the road and after 200 yards turn right along Cove Road to regain the shore.

The car park is a few minutes stroll along the shore to the left, but an alternative route which is not much longer starts just through the gate. A narrow walled track keeps above Red Rake to enter open fields of Bank House Farm National Trust land. Directly ahead through a couple of fields is Silverdale village. Gain the road at a sign in the top left corner of the field, turn right along the lane to the shore car park.

3. A circuit from Crag Foot - Yealand Conyers, Leighton Hall, Leighton Moss, Silverdale Green, Woodwell, Heald Brow

6³/₄ miles
2¹/₂-3 hours

A very pleasant walk which encompasses some lovely woodland paths, the park of Leighton Hall and the reed beds of the Leighton Moss Nature Reserve. Allow extra time to browse round the permanent exhibition centre at Leighton Moss.

Start: The route is described from Crag Foot, but the circuit could be done equally well from a number of other points - Leighton Moss, Silverdale station or the Coach Road.

Between Crag Foot and the level crossing, the Warton-Silverdale road crosses the deep stream of Quicksand Pool. There is enough space to park on the left just before the bridge.

Walk on the road towards the collection of cottages at Crag Foot, dominated by an ivy-clad chimney - the remains of a pumping station for a land drainage scheme which started around 1830. It also operated a saw mill. The embankment which was built to keep out the sea is clearly visible and our walk circuit finishes along it.

At the road corner take a lane on the left towards Moss House Farm, then another lane on the right. Turn left almost immediately into a wood. At its end cross the field diagonally right and at its top end turn right on a rocky track in a strip of light woodland between

Crag Foot

49

A CIRCUIT FROM CRAG FOOT   Walk 3

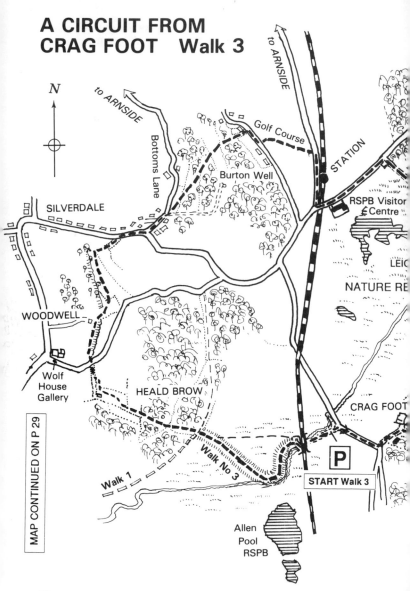

N

to ARNSIDE

to ARNSIDE

Golf Course

Bottoms Lane

Burton Well

STATION

RSPB Visitor Centre

SILVERDALE

LEIG

NATURE RE

WOODWELL

Wolf House Gallery

HEALD BROW

CRAG FOOT

P

START Walk 3

Walk 1

Walk No 3

MAP CONTINUED ON P 29

Allen Pool RSPB

50

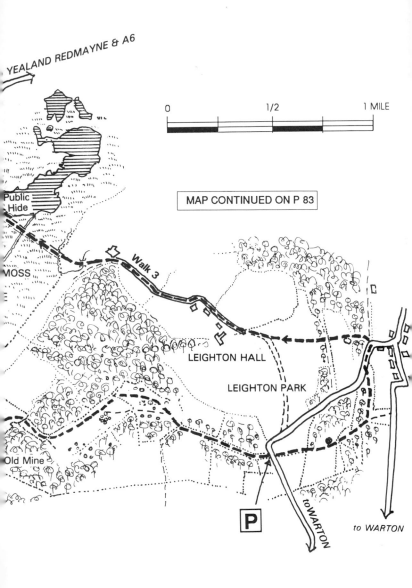

YEALAND REDMAYNE & A6

0   1/2   1 MILE

Public
Hide

MOSS

MAP CONTINUED ON P 83

Walk 3

LEIGHTON HALL

LEIGHTON PARK

Old Mine

P

to WARTON

to WARTON

51

denser woods. Bear left at junction, through a gate and go along the top edge of the wood - which contains some old mine shafts, relics of the copper and haematite mines which tunnel under these woods. See notes on page 18. Pass below a circular clump of trees and over a stile leave the prominent wall-side path and go diagonally right to the top edge of the field along a slight track which becomes more defined as it turns up the hill in a pretty wooded dell. Over a slit stile at the top, turn left to join a rough lane which descends gradually to the Coach Road. (There is space for car parking here.)

Cross the road and go through the field ahead to a rough track over

the crest of the hill. Continue in the same line past a limekiln. It is a fine example and still in good order. Limekilns were generally built between 1750 and 1850. The massively built rectangular construction housed a tunnel-like bowl where limestone was alternated with charcoal or timber - easily available in the area. It was left to burn for several days, and the resulting lime used for spreading on the fields or for making mortar.

Our path is descending towards Yealand Conyers, but at a slight rise, just before a large stone wall, take a left fork on a less well-defined track. This keeps just above the wall, through hawthorns,

Leighton Hall

over a stile to a clearing where there is an attractive view over Yealand Conyers. In spring the woods are alive with birdsong which does its best to drown the hum of the motorway not too far away.

Join a tarmac lane for a few yards, turn right on it, then left at a sharp bend into the edge of a fine beech and oak wood. There are several tracks but we are aiming for a gap on the hilltop skyline to the left. First, it is worth seeing a hollow straight ahead. This has a cemented water-catchment above it, and there is another at the top edge of the wood, reminders that water is a precious commodity in a limestone area.

There is a curious mound on the edge of the field at the top of the hill. This is known locally as the 'Summer House' and consists of a solidly built, circular base topped by a grassy mound with the remains of a stone building on its top.

Go across the field, through a blue gate to a fine terrace of beeches which overlook the grounds of Leighton Hall. The view is so stunning that two seats have been provided to enable the visitor to enjoy it leisurely - although a gale-blown tree has almost demolished them. Directly below, is the white stately home of Leighton Hall, cradled by woods. Morecambe Bay glints behind the Silverdale hills and in between lie the brown (or green according to season) reed beds and silvery meres of Leighton Moss. Our route across the causeway can be easily defined.

The right of way through Leighton Park lies a little to the right by the line of electric poles. Descend to the tarmac lane in front of the hall, turn right along it, past the Home Farm and in half a mile reach Grisedale Farm. This is built on the edge of the low-lying moss. Just through the gate ahead fork right to join a lane which curls right to enter the Leighton Moss Nature Reserve. The Causeway stretches in a dead straight line ahead, bordered by head-high reeds and willows. About half-way across a large mere can be seen on the right. The long timber hide on the right is open to the public and gives a good view of the birds on the mere. Informative posters and pictures enable even casual bird watchers to identify the various birds and a note-book is provided where otter sightings are recorded. From January to June you are quite likely to hear the booming call of the bittern, a bird which is quite rare but breeds at Leighton Moss. You will be very lucky to see one, as its vertical striped body is ideal camouflage amongst the reeds. A pair of marsh harriers, large birds of prey, hunt over the reeds. Another resident bird at Leighton Moss is the rare bearded tit, a small grey bird with a distinctive black flash under its chin. You are quite likely to see them amongst the small trees and reeds which line the The Causeway. Leighton Moss is the only place these three species breed in the north-west. In periods of wet weather The Causeway floods and becomes a shallow wade.

Emerge from the reeds onto the road, turn left and in 350 yards reach the RSPB Visitor Centre on the left. There is a well-stocked gift shop and a permanent exhibition; well worth an hour of anyone's time. The Leighton Moss Reserve was established in 1964 and in 1974 the RSPB bought 6,000 acres of the marshland on the edge of Morecambe Bay between Hest Bank and Arnside Point to improve one of the most important bird reserves in the country.

Many walkers who are not specially interested in birds do not realise the significance of the intense activity which takes place on the estuary and the moss, for it is of international importance. Many birds use the estuary as a staging post on a long migratory journey - birds such as greenshank and whimbrel on their way from the Arctic

Bittern

to Africa. White wagtails pass in spring on their way to Iceland, whilst pink footed geese fly over from their breeding grounds below the icecaps of Central Iceland. Waders, such as the dunlin, redshank and oystercatcher winter on the estuary. Many dunlin leave in spring for Scandinavia and Russia. Shelduck, which breed in the area, often inland in rabbit holes, make a strange moult migration to Heligoland in Germany, returning in mid-September.

Occasional rare visitors, like the osprey, promote great excitement on the 'twitchers' grapevine, and Leighton Moss is invaded by keen bird watchers from a wide area.

Apart from the public hide on The Causeway, access to the other hides is free to RSPB members, but a charge is made to non-members.

To continue the second half of our walk, turn left on the road outside the RSPB centre, then right to Silverdale station (restaurant open lunch times). One hundred yards past the station take a path left across the beautifully trimmed greens of Silverdale golf course. This is the most dangerous part of the walk; akin to crossing a military firing range. Having safely weathered the artillery, turn right on the lane at the far end and after 50 yards, on the brow of the hill, take a path left, signed 'The Green' between houses. Almost immediately you enter a tangled rocky wood and the nearby houses could be miles away. Descend a flight of steps and cross a clearing. There is a footbridge over water flowing from Burton Well on the left. The water sinks again a few yards into the woods. Enter woods again and mount a rocky path, slippery when wet or masked by leaves. Just before the first house of Silverdale Green, note an overgrown little quarry on the left - a sure sign of a nearby limekiln in Bottoms Lane. At Bottoms Lane turn left and soon join the busier Silverdale Road. Go right along this for 150 yards when a lane is seen on the left, signed 'Woodwell.' Follow the broad lane to a stile, continue by the side of a field to enter a strip of woods on the edge of a steep scarp. Again, despite the proximity of the village, the woodland walking is delightful with no sign of habitation. The path goes left and gradually descends through woods to a clearing, where a road and building is visible. Just before the road, descend into a pleasant wooded dell and cross a stile. Fork right on a rocky path to the edge of a line of small crags. There is a cliff top path but this misses a highlight of the walk. Descend a steep path down the face of the cliff, where steps have been

Woodwell

cut into the rock, to reach a rectangular pool. At the base of the cliff is a stone trough which catches water emerging from the roof. This is Woodwell, once the main water supply for the village and a drovers' watering spot. The rock strata is such that water falling on Warton Crag runs down the dip of the underlying rocks to collect under Leighton Moss before being forced up on the Silverdale side to emerge at various springs.

The observant may spot the shy hawfinch, especially in winter when flocks come to Woodwell to feed on cherry stones and beech mast. The birds gather in the tree-tops above the path. Continue along a path which runs parallel to and below the tangled line of low limestone crags, which seem to be losing the battle with vegetation. Trees entwine the rocks or sprout from unlikely points on the crag face, whilst ivy and moss creep along the crag surface endeavouring to cover all the indecently bare rock. A short rise joins the cliff top path and the road.

If time permits, Wolf House Gallery lies only 200 yards along the road on the right and is well worth a visit. The house itself derives its name from the wolf emblem on the Fleetwood family coat-of-arms carved above the front door. Now it is an interesting craft centre and art gallery with paintings by several well-known local artists, wood carvings, pottery and all manner of tasteful products - including some of the best coffee and home-baked goodies in the café. Make sure you visit the art gallery upstairs where there are various special exhibitions during the year.

Almost opposite the Woodwell path is a sign 'Heald Brow.' Follow a narrow track between wall and hedge - but not all the way, for at the far end the snicket is blocked. Instead, go left into a field and continue through a gate. Go diagonally left across a field with a new barn on the right, to the wall. Follow this left to a stile to the woods on top of Heald Brow. Views are restricted by the trees but there are glimpses of the estuary and Warton Crag ahead. A rocky path descends through thickets of brambles and gorse, with a final tricky descent which can be slippery if wet. Our destination is obvious ahead - the crest of an embankment, reached through a stile on the right. Salt marshes lie to the right and the high water mark lies perilously close to the embankment top. As the path curves left note the pool straight ahead - this is Allen Pool, the most recently excavated by the RSPB to encourage birds. There is a hide open to RSPB members only.

Cross the eerily-named water cut of Quicksand Pool and turn left under the railway bridge and to your car.

Bearded Tit

The first terrace on Warton Crag

4. Warton Crag Nature Reserve
2 miles
1½-2 hours

Warton Crag is the most southerly of the wooded limestone hills so typical of the area and the most familiar landmark to travellers on the motorway. A map of 1590 is reputed to show an Armada beacon and its summit also bears evidence of an ancient hill fort. The prominent limestone scars are popular amongst rock climbers - even the crumbling main quarry which takes a large unsightly bite out of the hillside. Warton village hugs the base of the hill and two roads run around the southern slopes towards Silverdale.

The village is well-known for its associations with the Washington family whose ancestors came to Warton from the north-east around 1350. An inscribed stone with the family coat-of-arms, which featured stars and stripes long before being adopted by the USA, can be seen inside the church, to where it was moved from the tower to prevent further weathering. The Black Bull Inn has obvious associations with droving days.

The Warton Crag Nature Reserve belongs to the Lancashire Trust for Nature Conservation, whilst another chunk of the hill is part of the RSPB Leighton Moss and Morecambe Bay Reserve. Signs at the

WARTON CRAG
Nature Reserve
Walk 4

Sketch Map

Signs at entry points indicate
permissive paths. Keep to
footpaths.
Lancashire Trust for
Nature Conservation.

Note: Not all the paths
shown here are rights
of way or permissive paths.
They are shown as an
aid to route-finding.

WARTON MAIN QUARRY
CAR PARK and PICNIC
AREA

In 1992 the Lancashire
County Council landscaped
the bottom of the quarry to
make an attractive picnic
area, with well surfaced
smooth paths.

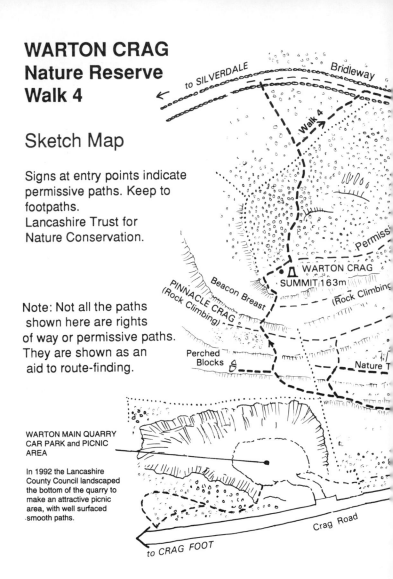

to SILVERDALE

Bridleway

Walk 4

Permiss

WARTON CRAG
SUMMIT 163m

(Rock Climbing

Beacon Breast

PINNACLE CRAG
(Rock Climbing)

Perched
Blocks

Nature T

Crag Road

to CRAG FOOT

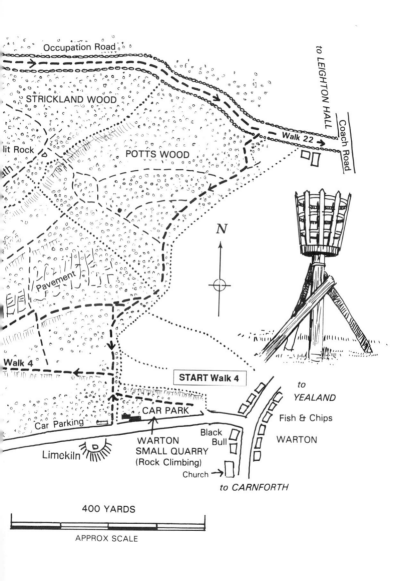

Occupation Road

STRICKLAND WOOD

POTTS WOOD

lit Rock

Split Rock

Pavement

Walk 4

Walk 4

Car Parking

Limekiln

to LEIGHTON HALL

Coach Road

Walk 22 →

N

START Walk 4

CAR PARK

WARTON SMALL QUARRY
(Rock Climbing)

Black Bull

Church →

to YEALAND

Fish & Chips

WARTON

to CARNFORTH

400 YARDS

APPROX SCALE

entry points indicate which are right of way and permissive paths.

It is an excellent place to explore and the sketch map shows other possibilities. Youngsters find the place exciting, with its crags, its maze of paths and varied walking. Views over Morecambe Bay are tremendous.

Start: The top road to Silverdale leaves Warton village close to The Black Bull. A few yards up the hill is the entrance to the Small Quarry car park. If this is full there is additional roadside parking 100 yards further up the hill almost opposite a restored limekiln.

A path leads through the quarry, a very popular rock climbing practice spot. Trees and rich vegetation hide all the nasty scars of quarrying and have transformed it into a very pleasant spot. In summer note the red valerian with its attractive red, pink and white flowers. This plant has established itself on the quarry walls from nearby gardens.

The quarry wall dwindles and at its top pass through a stile and turn right on the path from the alternative parking. Take the path left almost immediately, at the start of a rising terrace by a couple of stones. The path rises gently along a series of parallel shelves on a rocky limestone scar, which facing south is an excellent place for plants. Tight clusters of tiny rue-leaved saxifrage decorate the grey stone. Early purple orchids sprout on the path edge. Soon the edge of Warton Main Quarry is reached, guarded by a wire fence. The impressive climbing face is invisible directly below. Go over the stile and in 20 yards the path swings right away from the quarry top, up a scar to a terrace. Go left to a pile of distinctive perched blocks which

Warton Crag

62

The Perched Blocks, Warton Crag

command a wide view.

Directly below is Carnforth marsh backed by Morecambe Bay. On the edge of the marsh is a line of slag heaps, relics of the old Carnforth Ironworks. The town of Carnforth is displayed like a map and its importance as a railway junction is well seen. Steamtown, the railway museum is a popular tourist attraction.

From the perched blocks retrace steps to a mid point between the blocks and a wall. Turn left on a small path through trees and mount a short scar. Opposite behind a curtain of trees is the Pinnacle Crag, another popular climbing spot named after a pinnacle at its left end. A climbers' path runs along the base of the rocks. The woods are full of primroses growing amongst the rocks and of course the purple

The Split Rock

Go over a stile to climb a steep rocky path which ascends the right edge of the scar. Behind, the view to the terrace and the perched blocks with Morecambe Bay is especially good, particularly if the blackthorn is in bloom. Ahead the path rises up Beacon Breast to the flat summit, which is guarded by a rim of slight crags and walls. Remnants of the old hill fort built by the Brigantes are not obvious and would only be seen by a trained eye. A rock platform on the left is a fine vantage point towards Silverdale. The summit is crowned by a facsimile beacon erected in early 1988 as part of the re-enactment of the warning of the Spanish Armada of 1588. The beacon is constructed to an ancient specification. Beacons of this type were located in coastal and estuarial settlements all over England manned day and night to warn the country of invasion. The celebrations in 1988 were hampered by low cloud and bad weather.

From the summit a path leads north on the left of the beacon into the woods and a complete change of character from the open scars and grassy terraces of the south face to sombre enclosed woods which clothe the gentle back of Warton Crag. Take the left fork of the path signed 'Crag Foot' and descend gently through the trees. The plants change to shade-loving - wood sorell and carpets of bluebells. Pass a notable old yew with a fine dense canopy, go through a gap in a wall and fork right - signed 'Coach Road Warton' (the left fork goes

The view from Heald Brow across the embankment to Warton Crag.
The RSPB Reserve at Allen Pool is seen.(Walks Nos 1 and 2)

Above: Wood garlic at Woodwell.
Below: An autumn high tide at Jenny Brown's Point

to the same lane, but is a little further). Continue to more open woodland with clearings of bracken amongst silver birch and limestone pavement. Join a walled lane, Occupation Lane, an old droving route which crosses the back of Warton Crag, and turn right along this. It is popular amongst horse riders and the path may be churned. Abundant vegetation creates a tunnel, the stone walls draped in places with honeysuckle.

After about 100 yards there is a track entrance on the right between stone gateposts signed 'Concessionary path Warton Crag.' However, we continue along Occupation Road, over a slight rise then a gradual descent. Just before reaching the road take a track right signed 'Concessionary path to Warton local nature reserve.' This is followed close to the edge of the woods with glimpses over Warton village and the chalet-fringed lake of Pine Lake resort with flat-topped Ingleborough behind. Re-enter Warton Crag Nature Reserve and continue to the path junction at the top of the small quarry and so back to the start.

The Warton Crag Nature Trail
1¼ miles
1-2 hours

This is a very short walk established by the Lancashire Trust for Nature Conservation and is restricted to Council owned land. An informative leaflet which describes the trail and flora in detail is available locally, or from the RSPB Centre at Leighton Moss. The trail is not waymarked and it is easy to confuse paths.

The first part of the route as far as the wire fence above Warton Main Quarry is as the preceding route, but just before the fence turn right along a small track, through a densely vegetated terrace. In summer the rosebay willowherb creates an attractive pink covering. Mount to another terrace where a path comes in from a stile on the left.

Directly above is the long line of white summit crags. Turn right and walk along the terrace well below the crags to join another path and continue along the edge of a small limestone pavement. Join another path, turn right along it. The path bears left again through shrubs and into woods. Turn right at the wall and continue back to the path junction above the small quarry.

Apart from the abundant and varied plants to be seen on Warton Crag, it is especially good for butterflies. Brimstone, small tortoise-shell and peacock can be seen from spring to autumn, whilst the rare holly blue has re-established in the area despite the chopping of its favourite holly habitat. Three species of fritillary: pearl bordered, small pearl bordered and high brown are common, their larvae feeding on the abundant violets.

* * *

5. Castlebarrow, the Pepper Pot and Eaves Wood Nature Trail
2^1/$_2$ miles
1^1/$_2$-2 hours

The straggling village of Silverdale is prevented from straggling even further northwards by a prominent forested hill crowned by a squat obelisk, the Pepper Pot. The hill has a broad top with several small summits, King William's Hill directly above Silverdale, the craggy wart-like Castlebarrow protruding from the surrounding wood and host of the obelisk, whilst Middlebarrow is the summit which lies on the other side of the hill overlooking Arnside Tower.

Eaves Wood, which covers the south side of the hill, was bought for the National Trust in 1976 and another small strip of woodland was bought a years later and a car park was constructed.

This walk is very popular and lies on well-marked, well-trodden paths, although some parts of the path lie over bare rock and can be slippery in wet weather. Care must be taken at such times not to twist an ankle in the rock crevices or grykes. The main path is broad and pleasant. Away from this, there are numerous tiny tracks which can be explored if you fancy an excursion into 'jungle country.' On such tracks you will encounter branches, undergrowth and mossy rocks with grykes to trap the unwary. You need a sense of adventure, for you soon become a prisoner of the path which leads you a twisting course to deposit you where it fancies and leaves you wondering where on earth you are.

The avenue into Eaves Wood

However, the route described avoids all pitfalls, and can occupy a short afternoon. Highly recommended in autumn when the woods are ablaze with colour.

CASTLEBARROW, MIDDLEBARROW
and EAVES WOOD
Walks 5 and 6

MAP CONTINUED ON P 40 and P 102

ARNSIDE TOWER

MIDDLEBARROW WOOD

Walk 6

Walk 2

MIDDLEBARROW

MIDDLER

Viewpoint

Pavement

HOLGATES
CARAVAN PARK

Walk 6

Walk 5

EAVES WOO

CASTLEBARROW

PEPPER
POT

Ruins
Steps

Walk

KING WILLIAM'S
HILL

Ruin

to ARNSIDE

ELMSLACK

Circle of
Beeches

to SILVERDALE

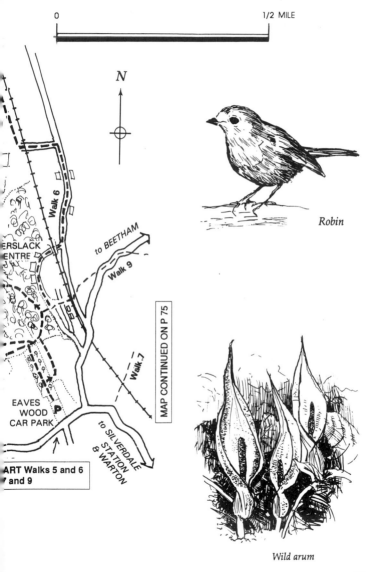

0   1/2 MILE

N

Walk 6

ERSLACK
ENTRE

to BEETHAM

Walk 9

Walk 7

MAP CONTINUED ON P 75

EAVES
WOOD
CAR PARK

to SILVERDALE
STATION
& WARTON

ART Walks 5 and 6
and 9

Robin

Wild arum

69

Start: From the National Trust car park which lies close to Waterslack Lane about half-way between the station and Silverdale. There is a collection box and a recommended voluntary fee of 20p per car. Enter the avenue of trees at the end of the car park and follow the white waymarks. Look out for and take a path right into an adjacent dell, turn left in this, through a stile at the top and into the woods.

Turn right to reach a broad lane which runs around the base of the woods. Right along this, then left up the hill where the buildings of Waterslack Farm Garden Centre can be seen through the trees on the right.

The path rises steadily past stately old oaks, pass through a break in the wall and continue uphill past two sharp bends to a junction. The short track on the right goes to a viewpoint across the workings of Middlebarrow Quarry and the Kent Estuary beyond. Continue on the main path which crosses a band of bare limestone pavement and levels out just below the crest of the hill. There are clearings in the woods and a good mix of trees, with yew, hazel and Scots pine. Pass a ruined wall and note the track which descends to the left. This is a short return which passes a notable circle of beech trees about half-way down the steep slope. We continue straight on past a long clearing. At the far end are the remains of a stone building and a flight of steps. This was built around 1830 to commemorate King William IV's accession to the throne. Go down the steps, pass through the wall on the right, cross a flat area of small trees, rise gently to a major path crossroads. A short, steep path on the left rises to the summit of Castlebarrow. The top is a flat rocky area covered with scrub and with the Pepper Pot perched on the left end overlooking Silverdale. This was built around 1887 to commemorate the Golden Jubilee of Queen Victoria's accession.

The view is exceptionally good, particularly if you have timed your ascent to coincide with the lowering sun on a winter's afternoon, when a golden glow spreads over the sparkling sands and channels of the bay - you will remember it for years! The coast from Barrow to Blackpool is visible, with the Lakeland Fells on one hand and the Pennines on the other.

Return to the wall below the steps of King William's Hill and continue down the steep slope. Take the right-hand path at a fork (stone seat), through dense woodland to reach another stone seat, which is an excuse for a short rest. Turn right at the next junction, left and left again on the path below. There are two parallel paths here, the upper which is more interesting is described. Pass a fine cluster of beeches, then a ruined cottage, past which the path descends gently (ignore the small track, keep left at fork), to reach the broad lane which runs around the base of the hill. Turn right then immediately left down the woodland ride to the car park.

A detailed leaflet which describes the nature trail is available locally. Several of the trees are labelled on the route.

The path in Eaves Wood crosses a limestone pavement   71

Arnside Tower with Arnside Knott behind

6. A circuit of Middlebarrow
3 miles
2 hours

Pleasant enough despite the lane walking and intrusive quarry scenery at the start.

Start at the National Trust Eaves Wood car park. Follow the start of the nature trail into the avenue towards Eaves Wood and look out for the white arrow pointing the way right into a shallow parallel valley. Go left up through a wall at its head, straight on into the woods with primroses and violets for company. As the houses of Waterslack appear through the trees, leave the nature trail and take a path right to a car park. Left along a narrow lane past the garden centre which is worth a browse, then go right at a gate 'Orchard Cottage.' Cross the railway and turn left along a tarmac lane.

This stretch of lane is unavoidable and goes to the entrance of the huge Middlebarrow Quarry, still working and a source of road aggregate. Cross the railway, then take a bridle path right into the woods along the base of Middlebarrow. The path bends sharp left at the corner of the wood where a path continues by the railway to Arnside.

Away from the railway the woods are more pleasant with many delicate redwoods. Arnside Knott's steep Shilla screes come into view and soon the stark remains of Arnside Tower. Go through a stile into the Tower's field and up by the wall side. The ruin is in a dangerous condition and should not be entered.

In the corner of the field go over a stile into woods again. Keep straight up the hill and suddenly emerge at the caravan site on Middlebarrow Plain, a shelf on the side of the hill. Turn right a few yards on a tarmac lane, then keep just above the children's play area on a small path which skirts the top of the caravan site as it rises through woods again.

After a level section, go through a wall and immediately turn left by the wall side. (Straight on is a quick level return to the car.) The path enters the National Trust Eaves Wood and becomes delightful.

Rise steeply by the wall until it levels. Pass a little clearing and bear right away from the wall into a hollow. There are several paths around here. Go straight on out of the hollow and along a little dell to a major path junction. A short, steep rise on the right leads to the flat, rocky top of Castlebarrow and the Pepper Pot overlooking the bay at its far end. The view is tremendous.

Retrace steps to the main path junction and turn right on the furthest of two parallel paths. It runs below a low line of rocks. Go through a wall and descend steps on the right. At a stone seat fork right through a derelict wall. Pass some fine beeches then bear left along a level shelf past another stone seat. Sharp bend right, then fork left after a few yards to bear left on the furthest of two paths. Follow this gently to the gap in the strip of woods where an avenue leads right back to the car.

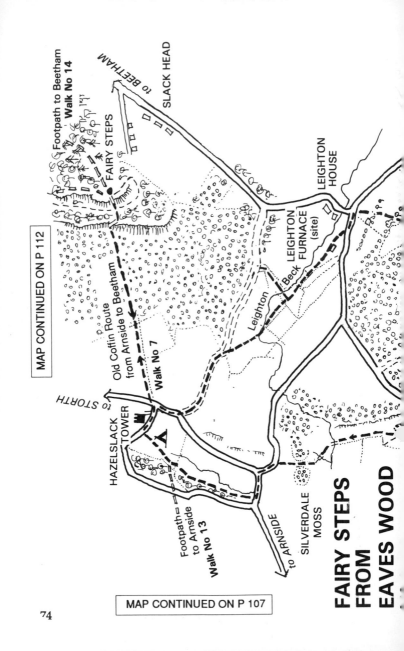

MAP CONTINUED ON P 112

Footpath to Beetham **Walk No 14**

FAIRY STEPS

to BEETHAM

SLACK HEAD

LEIGHTON HOUSE

LEIGHTON FURNACE (site)

Leighton Beck

Old Coffin Route from Arnside to Beetham

Walk No 7

to STORTH

HAZELSLACK TOWER

Footpath to Arnside **Walk No 13**

to ARNSIDE

SILVERDALE MOSS

FAIRY STEPS FROM EAVES WOOD

MAP CONTINUED ON P 107

74

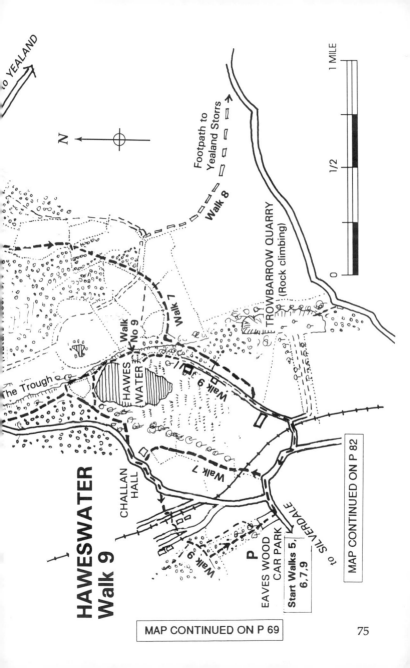

HAWESWATER
Walk 9

TO YEALAND

N

Footpath to Yealand Storrs

Walk 8

TROWBARROW QUARRY
(Rock climbing)

Walk 7

Walk No 9

The Trough

HAWES WATER

Walk 9

CHALLAN HALL

Walk 7

MAP CONTINUED ON P 82

EAVES WOOD CAR PARK

Start Walks 5, 6, 7, 9

Walk 9

to SILVERDALE

MAP CONTINUED ON P 69

1 MILE

1/2

0

7. A circuit from Eaves Wood car park - Haweswater, Hazelslack, Fairy Steps - return round Gait Barrows
6 miles
3-4 hours

A delightful varied walk which includes a good mix of woodland and clearing. Fairy Steps makes a fine climax.

Start: From the Eaves Wood car park east of Silverdale village. Turn left on the main road towards the station and after about 100 yards at a slight bend look for an unsigned path on the left. Keep close to the side of a wall, cross the railway and continue towards Challan Hall, visible through trees ahead. On the right is a good view of Trowbarrow poking its rocky head above the trees, and the flat marsh of Haweswater Moss.

Go through a gate and pass the left side of Challan Hall to reach a road. Turn right along this for 50 yards, then fork right at a descending forest lane. A bright red patch of eroded rock on the left of the path denotes the presence of haematite. Haweswater is now visible through the trees on the right. It is worth diverging from the main track at a curious ruined stone building where a path leads to the reed beds at the head of the lake. Haweswater is a shy lake, hidden by trees and tucked away from roads; indeed most visitors to the area are unaware of its presence. Unlike its big brother in the Lake District, it is small, but quite deep (about 100 feet). The surrounds of the lake are protected by the Lancashire Trust for Nature Conservation. At a public watering place on the opposite side of the lake cattle drovers used to water their herds.

Back on the main track continue past the head of the lake to an open field, Clay Holes, which provided a source of clay for pottery in the Middle Ages. The lane skirts the edge of the field and just before it bends right take another track which leads left into the woods. This track runs through a shallow glade of coppiced hazels with a long line of low crag for company on the right. This crag is the line of The Trough and marks one of the most prominent faults in the area. It starts just south of Trowbarrow and runs almost due north for 1½ miles. Our path stays close to it for the next half mile.

Cross a road and continue (footpath sign) along a smooth woodland lane. At a clearing veer diagonally right to another smaller lane with the crags of The Trough on the right. We have emerged from the woodland now and Arnside Knott is seen across the moss. Arnside Tower stands starkly on the skyline and Middlebarrow Quarry serves to remind what lies beneath the thin veneer of trees and stony soil. The lane becomes blocked by trees, so take to its top edge and cross tiny Leighton Beck at a footbridge. Cross the field diagonally left to another bridge and just after bend right to a gap between two clumps of woodland. The road is just beyond. Turn left and keep left at a road junction to another junction about 200 yards on. In the corner on the right is a path signed 'Hazelslack.' This keeps to a low

Since this sketch was made, it is much tidier with a new gate and stile

77

Hazelslack Tower

limestone ridge, fringed with gorse and trees. Go through a stile by a gate where Hazelslack Tower comes into view ahead. Join a farm lane, through the pleasant camping site, turn right on the tarmac lane to the Tower.

It is worth viewing the squat ruin of Hazelslack Tower, a pele tower built in 1375 to give the local inhabitants a safe haven from marauding Scots. It conforms to the general pattern of thick walls and three storeys. Cattle were kept in a stockaded area around the tower.

Opposite the farm a sign points the footpath to Beetham and the Fairy Steps. The path takes a straight course towards the wooded hill, at first through meadows, then into the woods, the domain of dark, spreading yews which sprout from crevices in the moss-covered rocks. At last the path deviates as it zig-zags to the foot of a crag barrier and mounts a hidden cleft - dramatic in retrospect as the path seems to end on its edge. Continue to a second barrier of crags, split by a narrower rift up which our 'path' lies. These are the Fairy Steps and it is said that if you ascend the cleft without touching the sides you are allowed a wish. Few adults will accomplish this successfully as the sides narrow towards the top, and the steps are polished into marble.

The open belvedere at the top invites a prolonged halt as befits the high point of the walk. It is a fine viewpoint across the Kent Estuary and Arnside Knott to the Lakeland Fells.

The path from Arnside to Beetham via Fairy Steps was a 'coffin route' until a church was built at Arnside in Victorian times.

To continue the walk it is necessary to return to Hazelslack, for although there is a short cut through the woods, this is not a right of way. At Hazelslack turn left along the road for 100 yards, then left along a bridle track signed 'Leighton Beck.' After 200 yards at a left bend there is a gate with a footpath sign. Cross the meadow to a tiny

Fairy Steps

footbridge over Leighton Beck. Continue in meadows along the valley bottom, on a gated track which becomes more pronounced.

Leighton Beck is the only reasonable sized stream in the area, and here the narrow valley with a fast-running stream proved an ideal site for the construction of a dam for a head of water to work the bellows of Leighton Furnace. The furnace was built in 1713 to make iron from iron ore. There was a plentiful supply of wood for charcoal and peat from the nearby mosses. The amount of local ore was small and most ore came from Furness across the estuary by boat, then pack-horse and cart from various points including the Cove at Silverdale. The furnace closed in 1810 and now very little remains. The path passes the slag heap and you can identify the dam and mill race. Of the buildings, only the fuel store remains, now a farm building.

Soon after passing a barn reach the road. Turn left to a road junction by the bridge, opposite which on the right is a sign 'Footpath to Yealand Storrs.' This path is not well marked and you have to aim for the gaps, stiles or gates. The first gap is slightly left in a band of trees, then cross a gap in a wall straight ahead at a second band of trees. Go straight across a broad, long meadow, through a gate, and as the field narrows and levels keep to the right edge of the field to a stile at the corner of a fence. This is the edge of the Gait Barrows Reserve, an area of outstanding interest to naturalists. Listen and you may hear woodpeckers and many other birds.

From the stile enter the glade on the right, go down it for 50 yards and right through a band of trees into a parallel glade. Keep diagonally right across into a third lower glade. The path becomes more distinct through trees close to the right edge of a wood to emerge onto a walled bridle path. Cross this, through a slit stile into the meadow, and still keeping close to the wall on the right pass an entry sign to Gait Barrows.

The circuit is almost complete for Trowbarrow's wooded crown lies straight ahead, and if you know where to look, Haweswater's hollow can be identified on the right. The path swings slightly away from the wall as it rises to the crest of the Trowbarrow ridge, to cross our old friend, The Trough. Just over the rise turn right for a few yards, then down left, just at the start of a low crag on the right. Turn left on the barely visible track which gradually improves as it descends to a stile. On the right a wire fence marks the domain of pigs.

The track becomes more defined as it leaves the dense woodland to emerge on the lane by some cottages. Follow the lane to the main road, turn right and soon reach the car park.

* * *

8. A circuit from Yealand Storrs, Cringlebarrow, Leighton Hall, Leighton Moss and Yealand Hall Allotment
5¹/₂ miles
2¹/₂-3 hours

This walk has a wide variety of scrub, open and dense woodland, park and meadow, with a crossing of Leighton Moss by the Causeway, which often floods in wet weather. At such times it is necessary to wade. The circuit could be made equally well from Silverdale station or Yealand Redmayne, or slightly longer from Eaves Wood car park.

The most convenient parking is found at the lane junction at Yealand Storrs - see sketch map and the walk is described from this point.

Start: Go towards Yealand Redmayne along the road for almost ¹/₂ mile to just over the highest point round a bend where a footpath sign (to Thrang End) left is seen. Opposite this on the right is the start of an unsigned path which we take, along a narrow strip of wood, past the old village pound then a path above the first houses of Yealand Redmayne to enter Cringlebarrow woods. Skirt the edge of a clearing, right, then rise into the dense woods. Go left at a junction and the path runs just below the tangled summit, becoming broader where another path is joined on the left. Descend into a clearing and pass the right-hand of two metal gates into woods again. Just before the road is reached at a corner turn sharp right up the hill to a gap where you find a curious stone mound with the remains of a summer-house.

Straight across the field go through a wicket gate to a fine avenue of stately beeches overlooking Leighton Hall, set in smooth parkland with the Silverdale hills and the bay of the Lakeland fells behind. There is a convenient seat from which to admire the setting.

The neo-Gothic facade of Leighton Hall was built in 1800, although the original hall was built in 1246. It is open to the public at restricted

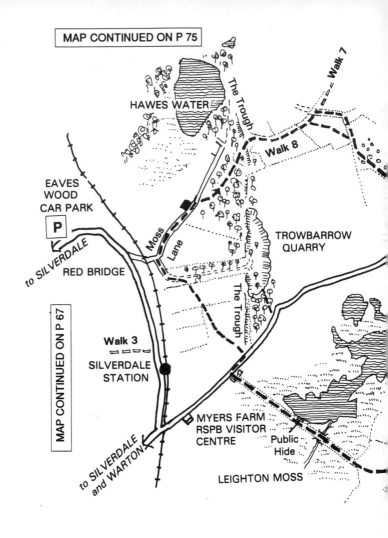

MAP CONTINUED ON P 75

HAWES WATER

The Trough

Walk 7

Walk 8

EAVES
WOOD
CAR PARK

P

to SILVERDALE

RED BRIDGE

Moss Lane

TROWBARROW
QUARRY

The Trough

MAP CONTINUED ON P 67

Walk 3

SILVERDALE
STATION

MYERS FARM
RSPB VISITOR
CENTRE

Public
Hide

to SILVERDALE
and WARTON

LEIGHTON MOSS

LEIGHTON MOSS & CRINGLEBARROW
Walks 8 and 10

82

0   1/2   1 MILE

to ARNSIDE

EALAND HALL
LOTMENT

ART Walk 8

P

YEALAND STORRS

Start Walk 10

N

BROW FOOT
FARM

YEALAND
REDMAYNE

Walk 10

CRINGLEBARROW

DEEPDALE

ISEDALE
RM

Walk 10

YEALAND
CONYERS

8

Walk 10

LEIGHTON HALL

Leighton Park

V

MAP CONTINUED ON P 51

83

times during the summer months.

The right of way through the park lies just to the right by a line of electricity poles and descends to the tarmac lane by the hall. Turn right along this past the Home Farm and the end of the lane at Grisedale Farm. Go through the gate ahead, bear right over a tiny bridge to enter the Leighton Moss Nature Reserve at the Causeway.

Between 1830 and 1917 Leighton Moss was drained by an ambitious pumping scheme to give fertile farm land. When the pumping ended it soon reverted to marsh, becoming an RSPB Reserve in 1964. Now there is an informative reception centre, shop and tea-room, several well-placed hides and walkways through the reed beds, which attract thousands of bird enthusiasts every year. The most notable rare residents are the bittern, the marsh harrier and the bearded tit. Otters also breed here and can often be seen at dusk playing in the meres. One of the most impressive sights for those with only a passing interest in birds is the evening display of starlings coming to roost amongst the reeds. The roosting starlings preferred Central Pier at Morecambe for several years, but appear to be returning to Leighton Moss. The sky is filled with twisting black specks of countless birds, swooping, rushing and finally dropping into the reeds - the noise is awesome. Birds of prey often wait on the fringe ready to strike. Apart from the Causeway and public hide,

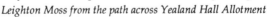

Leighton Moss from the path across Yealand Hall Allotment

access is by permit, available from the reception centre for a small fee. Free for members of the RSPB.

The Causeway cuts a shoulder-high course through the reed beds and its willow fringe. Past the main dyke there is the public hide, which you are welcome to enter, have a sit down and identify the various ducks on the mere with the aid of helpful pictures. The Causeway is a good place to hear the booming call of the bittern between January and June, although you will be very lucky to see one. At the main road the reception centre lies a few hundred yards left, but our path lies right, along the road for 100 yards then left at a sign 'Red Bridge Lane.' Note at the edge of the wood the start of The Trough - a curious natural rock feature on a fault line which runs right along the top of Trowbarrow, past Haweswater and Hazelslack to finish near Storth. Several of the walks in this book meet it from time to time. The first part almost looks like a quarried lane, tempting but inadvisable to explore as it is not a right of way.

Cross the field to a stile in the far corner by a telegraph pole. Another slit stile gives access to the strip of woods which enclose the quarry road, turn left and soon reach Moss Lane. Go right along this for 300 yards to just past a row of cottages on the left (Red Hall Cottages). Just past this is a stile into the field on the right. Cross the stile and follow a path just above a pig farm which at first keeps

parallel to the lane then diverges into woods. The top of Trowbarrow Quarry can be seen peeping over trees on the right. This quarry was one of the first in the country to produce tarmacadam around 1904. Since quarrying stopped in 1965 it has become popular with rock climbers although access is not officially allowed.

Pass a slit stile and continue in the same gently rising line just below the crest of the hill to a fork at a wall. The left path leads only to dead ends, so take the right over the hill crest and descend into a meadow. Keep close to the wall and pass an opening which leads onto the Gait Barrows Nature Conservancy Reserve.

Gait Barrows was made a reserve in 1977, chiefly to protect the limestone pavement which is one of the most important in Britain. It is traversed by two public paths which do not go near the interesting pavement and are difficult to link into a circuit without lane walking. If you are passing in summer the open meadow will be a tall sea of gently waving grasses richly decked with yellow, white, pink and purple flowers - a reminder of how meadows used to look before the advent of modern farming methods. If you specially want to visit the Reserve apply for a permit to the Reserve Warden, Orchard Cottage, Waterslack, Silverdale, Carnforth.

Continue in the field outside the Reserve to a lane, turn right and where it swings left continue through a gate to enter an area of brambles, small trees and clearings. Past another gate it develops into a bridleway along Yealand Hall Allotment. There are glimpses through the trees of silvery meres at Leighton Moss, whilst the thick woods of Cringlebarrow lie ahead.

The rough road passes through light woods of gnarled yews and holly to emerge on the road at Yealand Storrs.

Shorter option from Yealand Storrs
A footpath which starts at the road corner by the first houses goes through meadows directly to Leighton Hall and misses some of the best bits of the walk.

❋   ❋   ❋

9. A circuit of Haweswater *(Map p.75)*
2 miles
1 hour
A very short walk which includes some lane walking. Start from the

Eaves Wood National Trust car park.

Start: Leave the car park left by the road towards Silverdale station. After ¹/₄ mile fork left on Moss Lane at Red Bridge. This lane passes several cottages fringing Haweswater Moss on the left. After ¹/₂ mile the tarmac ends. Continue on the path ahead through woods to end at the edge of the lake, here defended by reeds. This is the important watering spot of cattle droving days. In June the marshy ground around the lake is full of pink bird's eye primrose and the woodland with ragged robin. Haweswater is a good place to see blackcap and garden warbler; birds which like the thick undergrowth of bramble and blackthorn.

Retrace steps a few yards to a stile and notice 'Haweswater Reserve. Lancashire Trust for Nature Conservation.' Cross the stile and follow the path by the edge of the wall to another stile at the entrance to the Gait Barrows Nature Reserve.

Gait Barrows was declared a reserve in 1977 to celebrate the Silver Jubilee of Queen Elizabeth II. It was established to protect one of the most important areas of limestone pavement in Britain, which is of exceptional botanical interest.

Our path does not enter the Reserve, but turn left and continue round the head of the lake, which is visible through its protective trees and reeds. A Haweswater Reserve path branches left to the water's edge, but keep on the main track which turns a horseshoe bend round a field which was an important source of clay for pottery making in medieval times. On the right is a 20ft-high rampart of rock, a small part of The Trough, the most important north-south fault in the area.

We are now on the return leg of the walk, and the broad track rises gently to emerge on the road just before Challan Hall; a large colour-washed house on the left. 200 yards further take a stile on the right and a narrow fenced track goes over a rise to a small lane. Twenty yards on the left a stile points the way across the railway by a small caravan park. Keep straight across a lane through a stile and diagonally left across a field. Waterslack Farm, now a well-stocked garden centre lies to the right. Go through a stile ahead into Eaves Wood. Bear left at a fork, keep left again through a slit stile and at the end of the wood rise right to join a broad track. Left on this to the car park.

*Cringlebarrow and Deepdale Woods
from Yealand Hall Allotment*

**10. Cringlebarrow and Deepdale Woods from Yealand
Redmayne** *(Map p.82)*
3¹/4 miles
2 hours approx.

An attractive little circuit with a mixture of dense woodland walking
and open parkland around Leighton Hall. Note that in mid-summer
the woods are too dense for comfort!

Start: About 100 yards from the north end of the village of Yealand
Redmayne where the Silverdale road bends, there is adequate verge
parking for a few cars at the edge of a narrow strip of wood. Just a little
further is a footpath sign 'Thrang End.' Our path starts opposite this
and is unsigned, but it takes a widening strip of dense woodland
between the road and a field. Go through a plantation and pass the
top side of Yealand Redmayne to enter Deepdale Wood, an attractive
mix of low limestone craglets, gently rising terraces and dense wood.
Through a gate keep straight on a broad path to a long clearing. Turn
right at its entrance on a small woodland path which skirts the edge
of the clearing. The path rises gently along one of the terraces,

bordered by brambles. Skirt the edge of a clearing and rise by mossy ivy-clad rocks into a tangle of small trees.

A junction is reached and our route lies to the left. (The right-hand path with a left turn after 30 yards is worth taking as a short diversion to the rocky crest of Cringlebarrow and a small clearing where there is a view over Storrs Moss to Silverdale and the Lakeland hills - quite a contrast to the enclosed woodland. Like looking through a window. A tortuous path along the jungle-like crest can be followed to the top of Cringlebarrow if so inclined, but most people will prefer to retrace their steps to the main path at the junction.)

The main path is broad enough to dispel any feeling of claustrophobia and the drone of traffic is a reminder of the nearby M6. The path lies parallel to and at a lower level than the summit ridge of Cringlebarrow, although various small tracks lead right into the dense thickets of yews which grow from mossy crevices in the rocks at this point. The woods are never dull with a wide variety of trees. Even in winter there is ample greenery from the yews, pines and the ivy which tenaciously entwine the trunks of many trees.

Continue straight along the main rutted path which descends gradually to meet another track coming in from Yealand Redmayne

The alternative path into the hollow of Deepdale - over the stile and up the hewn steps into a dense tangle of woods

on the left. Go through a clearing where another track into Deepdale branches right (see drawing). Enter woodland again, through the right-hand iron gate and just before the road is reached, strike sharply right up the hill to a gap at the top of an open field.

There is a curious circular stone mound with steps to a ruined building. Cross the field and go through a wicket gate to a stately avenue of beeches which overlook the neat parkland around Leighton Hall. The view is exceptionally good and seats are provided to admire it, although I suspect it will be of more use to those doing the walk the other way round having puffed up the steep slope from the Hall. One of the seats just escaped damage from a gale-blown tree.

The path is hardly visible on the lawn-like slopes, but follows the line of electricity poles just on the right to gain the tarmac road in front of Leighton Hall.

Leighton Hall is open to the public at restricted times from May to September. It is a curious building with a toy fort look, its white battlemented tower usually flying the flag of St. George, a landmark for many miles. Leighton Hall was first built in 1246, destroyed by soldiers in 1715 and rebuilt in 1760. Its white neo-Gothic facade was added in 1800. It was the seat of the Gillow family for many years, well-known in the retail furniture business. It is noted for falconry and the tethered falcons can sometimes be observed in the grounds of the Hall. Draw your own comparison with the birds on nearby Leighton Moss. In 1990, the attraction is 'free-flying eagles.'

Turn right along the tarmac lane for a short way until opposite the Home Farm where a rutted track crosses fields on the right to enter the base of Deepdale Woods. The track breasts a rise to reveal a broad semi-circular hollow, its base full of slender birch. The map marks a small pond in the hollow, but only in wet periods is it significant, when the lack of an outlet allows the swamp to enlarge.

The rutted estate track swings into the back of the hollow - we take a more attractive path on the left flank which ascends steeply in company with a long, low line of crags, whose rocks are sheltered by a coating of moss and a canopy of yews. Breast the crest, go through a gateless gateway and join the path we came on. Turn left and return to your car.

ARNSIDE

Arnside was a small fishing village and port before the building of the railway. Many of the small coastal villages were important ports as the roads were so poor that most internal trade went by sea or river. Until 1854 Arnside had its own customs house. In 1847 the Furness Railway was built to cater for the boom in iron and later, shipbuilding.

The construction of the railway viaduct, with its 50 pillars was a remarkable feat of engineering, carried out by Alexander Brogden and James Brunless. In order to find a firm foundation in the sands, hollow iron piles were driven down and water forced down the

interior under pressure. This caused the sand and water to boil up inside the piles and they sank further. More piles were fixed to the originals and the process repeated until the foundation was considered firm enough.

The construction of the viaduct resulted in the reclamation of a large area of land on both sides of the estuary. Arnside declined rapidly as a port, as its channel silted. Now it is a popular little holiday resort and a favourite retirement village due to its mild climate and sheltered position on the slopes of the Knott.

Arnside

ARNSIDE AND THE COAST
Walk 11

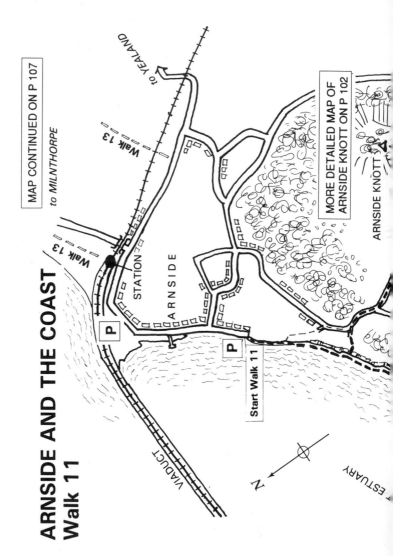

MAP CONTINUED ON P 107

to MILNTHORPE

to YEALAND

Walk 13

Walk 13

MORE DETAILED MAP OF
ARNSIDE KNOTT ON P 102

ARNSIDE KNOTT

STATION

A R N S I D E

P

P

Start Walk 11

VIADUCT

N

ESTUARY

MAP CONTINUED ON P 41

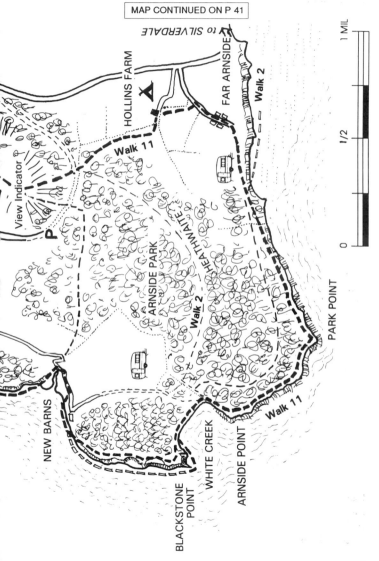

to SILVERDALE

HOLLINS FARM

FAR ARNSIDE

Walk 2

Walk 11

View Indicator

P

ARNSIDE PARK

HEATHWAITE

Walk 2

PARK POINT

NEW BARNS

BLACKSTONE POINT

WHITE CREEK

ARNSIDE POINT

Walk 11

1 MIL

1/2

0

95

11. Around the shore from Arnside to Far Arnside - return over Arnside Knott

5 miles
2-3 hours

This walk is the most rewarding of all the paths around Arnside for it includes both the shore, with its limestone craggy fringe and wooded paths, and the fine viewpoint of Arnside Knott, at 522 feet, the commanding height in the area. The coastal path between White Creek and Far Arnside is particularly special, surely the finest bit of coastal footpath in the whole of north-west England? The walk can be attractive at any time of year, especially in spring when the woodland flowers are appearing and the bright yellow gorse demands notice. It is a walk to be savoured. Allow yourself time to notice the many remarkable fossils in the limestone rocks by the path, time to watch the birds which feed on the vast expanse of sands left by the receding tide, time to enjoy to the full the views across the estuary to the Lakeland hills.

At very high tides it is not feasible to walk along the shoreline all the way, but at the key points affected by high water - particularly around Blackstone Point, there are cliff top paths which provide a safe alternative. The best time to start the walk is on a receding tide. Some parts of the walk are rough and pebbly.

Start: At the end of the promenade in Arnside there is a parking area which quickly becomes filled. A concreted walkway continues from the promenade along the edge of the shore, which can be a bit messy after a high tide. Immediately past the coastguard station, you will see a broken crag on the left. Notice the fault in the rocks where the horizontal beds are broken. Here the movement of the fault has dragged the surrounding beds out of the horizontal.

The concreted walkway turns up some steps and into a narrow strip nature reserve, at the far end of which are some informative notice-boards which show pictures of the birds and flowers commonly seen in the area. Regain the shore and continue along the pebbly edge. Just before reaching a bay, you should see some interesting fossil brachiopods in the rocks by your feet - Gigantoproductus - a fossil bivalve which looks like half a tennis ball protruding from the rock. These are quite common along the shore. One valve was spherical, the other flat. Look out for a fossil coral, lots of tiny crinoids

96

Above: The holly blue butterfly has re-established in the area.
Below: The Pepperpot, on Castlebarrow, is a fine viewpoint over the bay. (Walk Nos 5 and 6)

Cliffs near Blackstone Point

- like tiny polo mints, before continuing round the bay. Some of the rocks glisten as though they contain myriads of tiny diamonds. These are calcite crystals.

Don't be tempted to take a short cut across the bay to the cottages opposite, New Barns, as the intervening creek is deep and nasty. Cross the creek at a bridge and regain the shore by the cottages. We are opposite the craggy wood-topped hill of Meathop Quarry across the estuary, long disused and now a haven for plant and wildlife. Along the shore we reach a little quarry and if the tide is high it is advisable to proceed along the cliff top path. Otherwise keep to the base of the crag at the edge of the sand. There are some specially good fossil corals to be seen and fossil burrows - worm tracks - in the roof of an overhang at about head height.

The cliff ends at a spit of limestone which thrusts out into the sand. This is Blackstone Point, once a landing spot for ships when the Kent Estuary was used for commercial shipping.

The views expand as we round the point and reach the attractive bay of White Creek. Woods clothe the edge of the bay and there is no sign of the caravan site that lies close by. Cross the edge of the pebble beach and at its end gain a path which rises to join a major path at a sign 'White Creek - Far Arnside.' Turn right along this and enjoy the

Circle of beeches in Eaves Wood (Walks 5 and 6)

next half-mile of wonderful cliff top path. We are just high enough above the sands to get extensive views - and to feel the exposure as the narrow path comes perilously close to the edge in places. It is perfectly feasible to walk this stretch of the sands, but the path makes a pleasant change, and after passing Arnside Point and Park Point it rises through a lush patch of wild daffodils to join a higher track. Turn right along this through a well hidden caravan site to a tarmac lane at the cottages of Far Arnside.

Blackstone Point

After 100 yards take a signed footpath left across a field to join another track at Hollins Farm. The Knott is well visible on the left and our path rises gently diagonally right from the farm to enter woods and the National Trust area at a path junction. The easy way back to Arnside is simply along the broad gentle path which curves round the steep western slope of the hill to the Knott car park. More rewarding is to continue over the summit of the hill by going straight

Far Arnside

across the broad track on a more sinuous path, which rises past a conveniently placed seat which commands excellent views, through scattered, windblown yews to a levelling where the path arrives on a shoulder. Keep on the crest of the hill, along the main path and note the knotted tree - one of a pair which were knotted in Victorian times and became a landmark of Arnside Knott. Now one has gone and the other is dead, unlikely to withstand winter gales for long.

The summit is quite close, return to the knotted tree and descend a steep path past it, go over a stile and cross a field to join the road from the car park. The large building directly ahead is Grange Hill Convalescent Home. Turn right along the lane and descend into the village. At a bend in the road a footpath is signed leading back to the shore, or continue along the road for another 100 yards before taking a footpath left to the shore not far from the end of the promenade.

12. Arnside Knott 522ft.

3¼ miles
2½ hours

One of the most popular spots in the area and justifiably so, for it is as good a viewpoint as any in northern England. Most of the Knott is National Trust property and is a network of paths. There is a large car park at the foot of the final steep slopes which allows easy access to the summit. Two nature trails start from this car park, but the trails are not waymarked. The route described is an attempt to include the best of Arnside Knott in a circuit, but there are so many paths that it is open to variation at the whim of the walker. The sketch map will show other possibilities.

Start: From the promenade in Arnside turn up the hill, then right on Red Hills Lane which leads onto Saul's Drive, past the large convalescent home onto the open fell and the National Trust car park. This is in a lovely setting fringed by trees.

Cross Saul's Drive and climb steeply up any of the gravelly paths through the trees to the toposcope which is set on the top of an open shoulder and commanding a fine view. Three finely engraved panels by Don Hinslie show clearly what can be seen if visibility is good. The Lakeland hills form a broad backcloth to the glittering Kent Estuary with its toy-like viaduct.

A path continues along the crest of the hill, through woods to emerge at a more open crest with a seat at a junction of paths. Keep on the main path for a few yards, then branch right along a much smaller track. This follows a balcony above steep slopes on the south-east side of the Knott and opens up the vast views on this side, across Morecambe Bay and the nearby wooded hills around Silverdale to the Pennines. The path undulates a little and is rocky in parts, exposed in others - particularly where it meets the top of the very steep Shilla slopes. A notice asks people to keep off the slopes as there has been considerable erosion damage. There is a bird's-eye view of Arnside Tower and the spring pool in the meadow to its left. Pass a minor path to the left, and continue until the path leaves the steep edge and swings left into dense trees. The path is in control - all you need to do is follow its twisting course and trust it is going the right way, and sure enough you pop out at a shrubby clearing with the trig

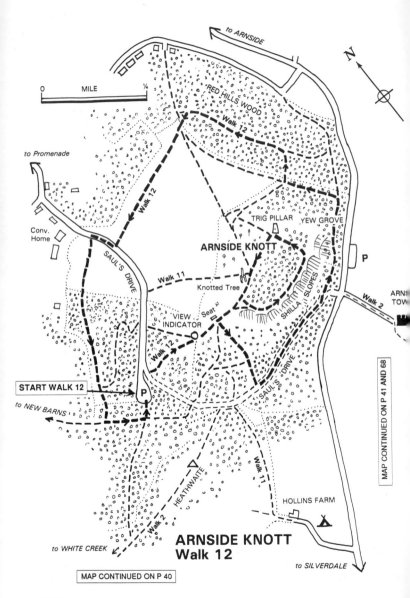

ARNSIDE KNOTT
Walk 12

MAP CONTINUED ON P 41 AND 68

MAP CONTINUED ON P 40

102

The knotted tree, Arnside Knott

point of the summit right in front. It is a junction of paths. Turn left
and reach a major path just above the tall, dead, knotted tree. Two
trees were knotted in Victorian times and became a notable landmark, now only one remains and that seems unlikely to survive

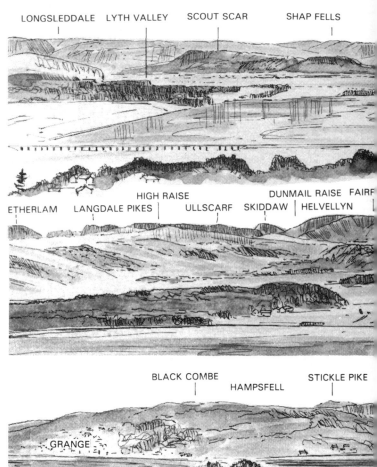

LONGSLEDDALE LYTH VALLEY SCOUT SCAR SHAP FELLS

HIGH RAISE DUNMAIL RAISE FAIRF
ETHERLAM LANGDALE PIKES ULLSCARF SKIDDAW HELVELLYN

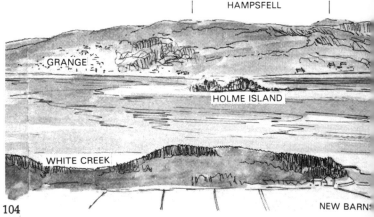

BLACK COMBE HAMPSFELL STICKLE PIKE

GRANGE

HOLME ISLAND

WHITE CREEK

104

NEW BARN:

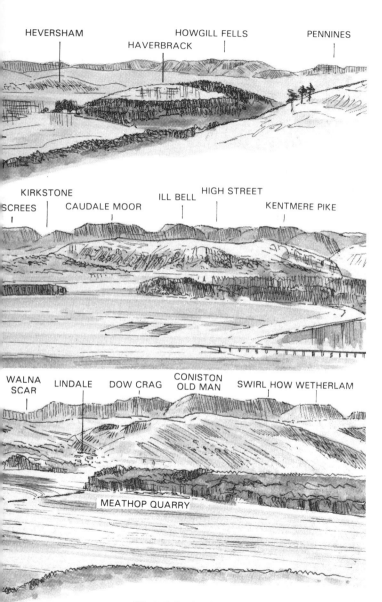

HEVERSHAM   HOWGILL FELLS   PENNINES
HAVERBRACK

KIRKSTONE
SCREES   CAUDALE MOOR   ILL BELL   HIGH STREET   KENTMERE PIKE

WALNA   LINDALE   DOW CRAG   CONISTON   SWIRL HOW WETHERLAM
SCAR   OLD MAN

MEATHOP QUARRY

The Lakeland Fells from Arnside Knott   105

many years. Follow the main path back to the seat we passed earlier. Turn left down the steep hillside on a path which passes a glacial boulder on the right to join the broad bridle path of Saul's Drive. Turn left and descend gently towards the road near Arnside Tower. Just before the road, take a smaller track which traverses the hillside on the left, below the steep Shilla slopes. Erosion is evident but now appears to be under control with the help of wire netting in key places. Shilla is a local word for scree. The path drops close to the road again by an old quarry. (There is a good parking spot near this point which can be used just as well for the circuit.)

Continue in the woods just above the road to a fine grove of yews. At a stone wall turn left up the hill, and just before a wall corner take a stile on the right into Red Hills Wood. Descend steeply a short way, then branch left on a smaller track which contours the wood to join another major track. Turn left and soon leave the woods into open pasture. Keep straight across on a gently descending track to the tarmac lane of Saul's Drive. Turn right for a few yards then a path leads left across another pasture and into the woods of the Larch Grove.

After a level stretch the path rises up steps and goes through a low stone wall. Either keep in the National Trust land in front of the wall, where a path rises through the woods to reach Saul's Drive just before the car park, or continue over the wall into more open ground to join a large path. This can be followed to Saul's Drive above the car park or any of the smaller paths branching left lead to the same place. An extension to the walk can be made over Heathwaite - turn right along the path instead of left to the car park (see map). This path leads to the clearing near the top of Heathwaite, whence a return is made along the crest left to Saul's Drive.

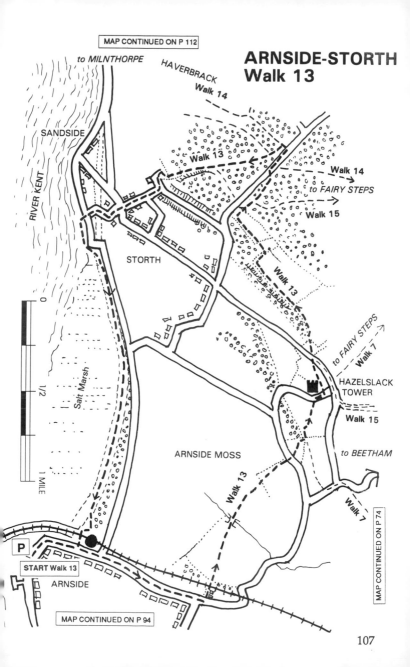

MAP CONTINUED ON P 112

to MILNTHORPE

HAVERBRACK

Walk 14

ARNSIDE-STORTH
Walk 13

SANDSIDE

Walk 13

RIVER KENT

Walk 14

to FAIRY STEPS

Walk 15

STORTH

Walk 13

Salt Marsh

to FAIRY STEPS

Walk 7

HAZELSLACK
TOWER

Walk 15

0

1/2

1 MILE

ARNSIDE MOSS

to BEETHAM

Walk 13

Walk 7

MAP CONTINUED ON P 74

P

START Walk 13

ARNSIDE

MAP CONTINUED ON P 94

13. A circuit from Arnside - Hazelslack Tower and Storth
5 miles
2¹/₂-3 hours

A pleasant circuit, quite varied in its mix of moss, woods and estuary scenery.

Start: Park in Arnside as near to the railway viaduct as possible. There is access to the marsh edge just below the viaduct, but if parking here make sure there are no high tides! Car parking on the front at Arnside can be difficult in summer.

Walk along the road past the railway station and continue straight on for half a mile where a path is signed on the left 'Footpath to Fairy Steps.' Go past the farm and over the railway to a broad green track across the open moss. Straight ahead is the wooded hill where Fairy

The old railway track makes a pleasant return to Arnside

Steps lie. Cross a lane and mount a small scar to a stile on the right just before the field corner. Turn left and left again immediately through another stile to join a farm lane which leads to Hazelslack Tower, well seen directly ahead. Right at the road, then left 'Storth' to the cottages by the tower.

It is worth looking at the squat remains of the Tower, not so tall and dominant as nearby Arnside Tower, but typical of the pele towers which were build around the fourteenth century as a safe haven from marauding Scots.

There is a stile immediately to the right of the cottage, turn left over it and cross the field slightly right to a footpath sign where a road is crossed. After 50 yards bear left from a cart-track to a stile in the wall corner in front of a strip of woods. The path follows the edge of this strip, with the broader woods of Fairy Steps a field away on the right.

On our left is a tangled limestone ridge which gradually gains height until it reaches quite impressive proportions under its cloak of moss and creeping trees. It is our old friend, 'The Trough' here named 'Longthroughs Wood,' the natural fault-formed north-south scar which forms so prominent a companion on several of our walks. The

path sticks close to the edge of the field, skirts the bottom end and enters a wood at a short lane. Just inside on the right there is a line of small springs which feed a tiny stream. This stream flows into the fields where we have walked, and is responsible for a large pool which forms there in wet weather, as the stream has no surface outlet. Leave the wood and enter another field. There is a path straight ahead to a lane, but it is preferable to go diagonally right to the edge of a plantation where a small gate with green sign 'Keep dogs on a lead' gives access to the dense woods. The path bears left then right at a small junction. Fork left after a few yards uphill, at a clearing and join a forest lane. (This goes up to the hill top and Fairy Steps, and could easily be incorporated into the walk.) Turn left on the lane and just before reaching the road take a small track on the right which joins the road higher up.

Turn right along the road and just over the brow of the hill meet a sign on the left 'Storth.' Turn left just through the stile and left again at a fork. Descend gently through the pleasantly rocky woods, keep left at a fork over a slight rise and descend again to join another path which rounds the edge of a small crag. Go straight on down the hill and a final sharper descent to a field. Cross this to a stile and join a lane.

Turn left a few yards to a junction with a road at Throughs House. Although the name is slightly altered, a glance opposite reveals the very end of The Trough, here an impressive ivy-covered crag.

Follow the lane right, past several houses of the scattered village of Storth, to fork left at the more compact village centre (shop). At the war memorial go right down Green Lane, cross the deep cutting of the old railway to join the busy coastal road. Cross it and after a few yards left, there is access to the grassy edge of the estuary.

There is a little track which passes a wire fence and mounts onto the old railway, now a pleasant grassy track which stretches away towards Arnside, whose houses clinging to the lower slopes of the Knott are plainly visible.

The sands and estuary channels are left behind as the railway swings in a big curve at the edge of the green marshes, here more channelled than those at Silverdale, and not as attractive. The seaward side of the embankment has been strengthened by a layer of wire netting to prevent damage by the high tides and strong winds.

As we near Arnside the channel swings close again. Go through a gate onto a gravel lane, with the station on the left. Cross the footbridge to join the road.

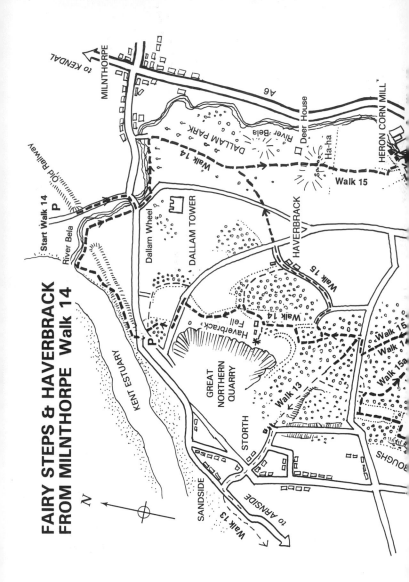

FAIRY STEPS & HAVERBRACK
FROM MILNTHORPE Walk 14

N

to KENDAL

MILNTHORPE

A6

Old Railway

Start Walk 14

P

River Bela

Walk 14

DALLAM PARK

River Bela

Deer House

Ha-ha

Walk 15

HERON CORN MILL

Dallam Wheel

DALLAM TOWER

HAVERBRACK

Walk 15

Walk 14

Haverbrack Fell

P

Walk 15

Walk 15a

Walk 1

KENT ESTUARY

GREAT
NORTHERN
QUARRY

Walk 13

STORTH

BOUGHS

SANDSIDE

to ARNSIDE

Walk 13

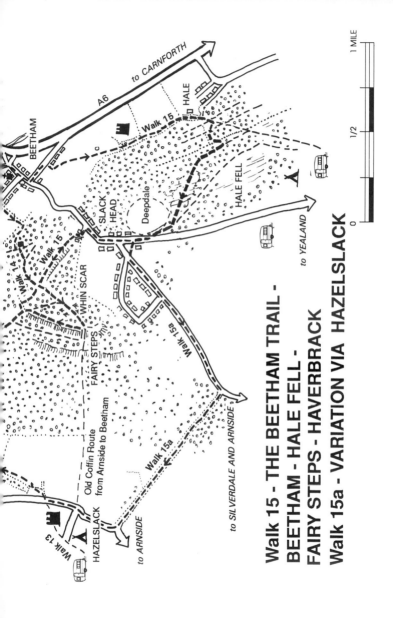

**Walk 15 - THE BEETHAM TRAIL -
BEETHAM - HALE FELL -
FAIRY STEPS - HAVERBRACK**

Walk 15a - VARIATION VIA HAZELSLACK

113

The bridge over the Bela into Dallam Park

14. A circuit from Milnthorpe -
Beetham, Fairy Steps, Haverbrack Fell and the Kent Estuary
5½ miles
3-4 hours

This varied walk includes a little of everything the area has to offer - parkland, woodland, limestone crag, estuary and a little bit of historical interest. The views from Haverbrack Fell surpass those from Fairy Steps and it is worth reserving a day of clear visibility for the walk.

Start: One could park in a "Pay and Display" car park at Milnthorpe, but a quieter start is to park on the little lane which runs along the side of the estuary. From Milnthorpe take the Arnside road for ³/₄ mile and turn right just before crossing the River Bela. A few hundred yards down this lane there is ample verge-side parking.

Return along the lane and cross the bridge to enter Dallam Park along the estate road. Turn left through the swing gate just before the house and continue by the side of the river until an older bridge is reached. Do not cross this but turn right and climb to the crest of a hill. Mallard often grace the pool below the bridge, the bright colours of the male contrasting with the more sober brown plumage of the female. Her bright blue wing flash is some compensation.

Dallam Tower can be seen to the right. It is the residence of the Wilson family, and was completed in 1720 on the site of an earlier house. The park was planted about the same time. Dallam Wheel is a notorious bend in the river nearer the house. In times of flood it forms a strong eddy and has claimed several lives. The Bela rises very quickly after heavy rain.

There is hardly any trace of a path and it does seem as though the walker is trespassing in the very private ground of a country house. However, there is a right of way and it is a justly popular local stroll. The earthwork on the hilltop marks the site of an earlier manor house. The deer house, built in the 18th century, comes into view in a hollow on the left and if you are lucky the large herd of fallow deer will be somewhere close by. These beautiful delicate creatures are not native to Britain and are believed to have been introduced by the Romans. The stags display their fine antlers as they stare guardedly at walkers. In winter the herd keeps close together. In summer, the bucks and does prefer to stay apart.

Go round the left side of the next rise to a stile in a fence. The wall

Heron Corn Mill

in a ditch is a ha-ha; a method of walling without spoiling the expanse of parkland. Cross the field to another stile on the left and squeeze through a slit stile onto a narrow green lane and car park. Directly ahead is the large and ugly complex of mill buildings which comprise the Henry Cook Ltd. paper mill. This was originally a corn mill and was converted to production of paper in 1788.

On our side of the river, facing the paper mill, is a much smaller, older building, the Heron Corn Mill. It is well worth visiting this if opening times coincide with your visit. (April-September, Tuesday-Sunday 11.00am.-5.00pm.) The mill ceased trading in 1955 but has been restored into a working museum. Corn has been ground on this site since 1220 although the present structure dates from 1750. The name derives from a heronry which existed close by until 1726. Herons can be seen frequently by the river. Inside the mill a high breast-shot 14ft. water-wheel powers four pairs of grindstones with water taken by sluice from the weir. Explanatory leaflets are available at the mill, café and paper-making museum.

Even if the mill is closed it is worth browsing round the exterior. The weir is merely an addition to a natural limestone shelf across the river, impressive in flood. At the head of the sluice there is another channel which vanishes into a natural limestone cave. This is where the original milling was done.

Return to the narrow green lane and follow it to a tarmac lane. Turn left along this until just before the first houses of Beetham village, where a path right is signed to Hazelslack. Go through a field and enter the woods. Turn right, keep above a wall, and the path swings uphill past a ruined cottage - in spring surrounded by a sea of snowdrops. Keep right of the cottage, left at a junction and right almost immediately uphill above the cottage, then right again on a broad track. Cross another track in a clearing and follow the signed path to Fairy Steps. Enter Dallam Tower Estate and note that walkers are asked to keep to the paths and to keep dogs on a lead. The crest of the hill is crowned by a stand of tall, dense pines, but just beyond the path bursts into a clearing on top of a band of steep crags. At first sight, the path ahead seems to end on the edge of the cliff, but a narrow cleft zig-zags down. These are the Fairy Steps - a highly polished fissure which is so narrow you would have great difficulty falling down, in fact at the top it requires a determined effort to move. Fairy Steps lies on the old 'coffin route' between Arnside and Beetham.

The grassy belvedere at the top of Fairy Steps deserves more than

Entering the narrow cleft of Fairy Steps

a brief passage, for if the visibility is good the view is worth absorbing in detail. Arnside Knott, the Kent Estuary and the Lakeland Fells are arrayed above the immediate collar of trees.

Our walk continues along the top of the crags, Whin Scar, to the right, but there is an alternative path which runs parallel along the base of the scar. It is certainly worth descending the Fairy Steps if only for the fun of it. Better views are obtained from the cliff top path. After crossing bare rocks it descends onto a broad track. Turn left on this to a grassy clearing where the alternative path joins. A signpost stands incongruously in the middle of the grassy sward.

Descend gently through the woods to a road, turn right for barely 50 yards where paths are signed to the left, one to Storth and one to Haverbrack. We want Haverbrack, which goes straight ahead into the woods. There is a confusing network of paths in this area, but generally we are walking the crest of the hill. Keep right at a fork, then left at a junction and right again in a few yards. Tracks in this wood are much narrower and less frequented than those around Fairy Steps. You feel that the path is in charge as it takes you on a surprise walk amongst the trees. The surprise soon appears as a gravel road is reached, for we are right on top of the huge New Northern Quarry above Sandside. (If you are not averse to a little industry, stroll down the road for impressive views into the quarry with its grey and ochre vertical cliffs.)

Where you emerge onto the road follow the edge of the fence right to join a broad track parallel to and out of sight of the quarry. Go left along this to an earth-banked building. A small path left leads to the top of the hill. The quarry is not obtrusive here and the views improve all the time. To the south and west lie the densely wooded Silverdale hills, and if you have walked many of the routes in this book you will be able to identify all the landmarks - from Warton Crag and Cringlebarrow, Trowbarrow and Middlebarrow to Arnside Knott. The green mantle cloaks all the presence of man.

Return to the building and continue on a good track to the right of it to a junction of tracks at the entrance to a wood. Go past a wall then immediately back left through a slit stile into a field on top of Haverbrack.

Now you know why a clear day is recommended for the walk as the

The Lakeland Fells from Haverbrack

CONISTON OLD MAN   WETHERLAM   LANGDALE PIKES   WHITBARROW SCAR

Limestone pavement on Haverbrack fell top - no access now due to quarrying

view northwards is revealed! The glistening ochres of the Kent Estuary sands lie directly below, whilst behind the limestone hills of White Scar and Whitbarrow, the Lakeland Fells fill the horizon. On the left Black Combe dips down to the sea, the Coniston Fells are the first of the high peaks, with the crags of Dow guarding the hollow where Goats Water lies. Next the Langdale Pikes poke proudly into

RED SCREES   HIGH STREET

RFIELD   KIRKSTONE   ILL BELL   KENTMERE PIKE
      PASS
       |

the skyline, whilst due north is the flat-topped Fairfield. We can see the entire horseshoe of its ridges, and the steep flanks of Red Screes which drops onto the Kirkstone Pass. Right again are the fells of the High Street range and Kentmere, and right again the Pennines. What a glorious view!

Keep along the field with the wall on the right. The path descends sharply - make for a stile and path sign just left of the field corner. Turn left along the narrow lane and after 150 yards right at a path signed 'Sandside.' Cross the busy coastal road and descend a flight of steps onto the old railway track. The character of the walk has changed again - to that of the estuary, for the path soon leaves the old railway and drops to the edge of the sands. Flocks of birds congregate on the sand flats, especially in winter. The path reaches the edge of the River Bela where it joins the Kent, and we follow its banks back to the road bridge. The railway embankment is visible across the river, but the intervening gap just a memory of the Bela viaduct. Turn left over the bridge, down the little lane back to the car.

Sandside and the Kent Estuary from the top of Haverbrack

Beetham Hall Farm

15. A circuit from Beetham (The Beetham Trail) - Hale, Hale Fell, Slack Head, Fairy Steps, Haverbrack and Dallam Park
5 miles
3-3¹/₂ hours

This walk crosses the woods of Hale Fell by a well marked path which crosses a fine limestone pavement. The Marble Quarries which are marked on the O.S. maps are sections where a layer or so of the pavement has been removed. The rock was a popular substitute for marble in Victorian times, for its attractive clouded appearance when cut and polished.

Walking the path over Hale Fell for the first edition of this book was like exploring the jungle. In four years the transformation is remarkable - from an exercise in navigation on tiny threads of path to a route so well signed that it would be difficult to lose the way. Perhaps the signs have been overdone!

After escaping from the confines of Hale Fell, a short return to the car can be made down the lane from Slack Head to Beetham, but it is pleasant to continue over the popular Fairy Steps. The alternative route walks mainly broad paths not covered elsewhere in this guide - apart from one section under Longthroughs Wood (Walk No.13).

Start: From Heron Corn Mill car park retrace steps along the riverside road to Beetham village. Turn right past the war memorial and church, left just past The Wheatsheaf Hotel. By some cottages on the right take a path signed 'Hale.' Go round the back of the cottages then diagonally across the field, keeping right of a lonely granite boulder

- a glacial erratic dumped by melting ice - to a stile in the top corner of the field (sign). Beetham Hall on the left, was a manor house which combined dwelling and defence. The pele tower is quite prominent and there are other remains of thick walls and several interesting remnants now incorporated into the farm buildings. It was another link in the chain of towers which were constructed around Morecambe Bay to repel marauding Scots in the 15th century. The overlordship of both Arnside and Beetham towers passed to the de Beetham family, but after the Battle of Bosworth in 1485, the new King Henry VII gave de Beetham's land to the Earl of Derby. In 1690 the towers were abandoned, lead was stripped from the roofs to repair other buildings and they gradually decayed.

Cross the stile into the wood. The path sticks close to the wall side (beware of nettles). Exit onto meadow and go below a small scar towards the first houses of Hale. Just before a wall an inclined grass track goes right and a path, fringed with great bell flowers, enters the woods. Join a well marked path which comes from Hale village, straight on (sign Limestone Link) to another path junction a little further. Turn right (yellow waymarks) and rise up a slight scar to a level shelf with another path junction and wall side. The right of way mounts left by the edge of the wall to the fell top. Pass through another wall onto level ground. Go along a track which joins a better one in about 50 yards. Turn right here (left joins the track to the caravan site) and follow a level but narrow path through dense vegetation for about 100 yards. Keep a sharp eye for a fork left, (waymark), where the trail ahead is barred by brushwood.

The path is easily followed amongst the trees and soon reaches a small clearing on the edge of a limestone pavement - Arnside Knott is seen poking above the trees - where the path appears to end. Follow waymarks across the bare limestone diagonally right to a short break through bush onto a second magnificent open pavement, seamed by two-directional crevices and water-worn rounded grooves. Go diagonally right again, in the direction of Slack Head whose doll-like houses can be seen thrusting through the trees. A short gap leads to pavement number 3, where a layer has been removed for quarrying. Turn downhill and enter the woods. A few years ago old margarine containers could be seen strewn around the trees and a glimpse right reveals the source - the ugly clearing which was formerly the local rubbish tip. Animals sought out the margarine containers to lick the

The path crosses a fine limestone pavement.
In the background are the houses of Slack Head

fat. A little further fork right and emerge onto the tarmac lane.

Having escaped from the claustrophobic, but interesting clutches of Hale Fell, it is pleasant to stroll easily along the lane right to Slack Head. One hundred yards down the road towards Beetham, turn left signed 'Fairy Steps and Storth.' Go right round a cottage, then bear left into woods along an almost level shelf to a path junction. Turn left - sign Fairy Steps.'

The numerous bolts on top of the crag are climbers' belay points - although in the crag to the north an earlier ring bolt is reputed to be an aid to hauling coffins on the trail from Arnside to Beetham.

Go right along the top edge of the crags with fine views over the estuary. The path becomes indistinct over rocks, then drops right through trees to join a broad path. Turn left on this into a clearing on Beetham Fell. Continue on the broad straight track to a road. Along the road right just over the brow of a hill is a path left signed 'Haverbrack' (ignore the Storth sign). Keep right at a fork then right again at the remains of an old signpost. Turn right at a rough lane and keep left at another junction on the edge of a wood overlooking a tiny tree-girt lake with Farleton Fell behind.

Pass the quiet hamlet of Haverbrack and 100 yards on a surfaced lane to a road junction. Cross a stile ahead and descend a park-like meadow to another lane with signposts.

We are indeed in Dallam Park, please do not stray from the rights of way described and make sure that dogs are under tight control. Go diagonally left through the stile to below the hilltop where the other right of way path from Milnthorpe is joined - a barely visible horizontal bank on the hillside. Go sharply right along this and cross a dip with the deer house on the left and aim for the centre of a clump of trees on the skyline where you are confronted by a stile on top of a sunken wall - a ha-ha - a popular device in landscaped estates to preserve the unhindered view. The Heron Corn Mill car park lies straight ahead.

15a. Alternative finish via Hazelslack and Beetham Fell
5³/4 miles (inclusive)
3-4 hours

This alternative uses an attractive combination of paths around the northern side of Fairy Steps.

From Slack Head go left on the road downhill for just over half a mile to a bridle path on the right, signed 'Footpath to Hazelslack.' After wet weather this track may be churned, but it provides pleasant walking at the base of woods, overlooking the meadows of Leighton Beck to another tarmac lane, where a turn right leads to Hazelslack.

About 200 yards past the farm and ruined tower, go through a gate right at a footpath sign. Ahead is a crown of trees on a slight ridge with a stile in the corner on the right. The path keeps to the edge of a long meadow, close under the scar of Longthroughs Wood, the continuation of the prominent north-south fault which cuts right through the area. Across the meadow rise the woods of Fairy Steps topped by a distinctive cap of conifers. The two scars near the hilltop can be distinguished amongst the trees. At the far end of the meadow enter a short strip of woodland, past a line of springs, to gain a second wood-lined meadow. Continue almost to the lane at its end, but turn right and enter the woods through a tall gate. Soon a broad woodland track is joined, up which turn right, past a small spring and dilapidated footpath sign. The broad track swings right and our path continues straight ahead, rising steadily past rocks and through two gates onto a broad grass clearing on the shoulder of the hill. There is an incongruous footpath sign stuck starkly in the middle. Turn right on a velvet-like turf path which we leave just before it enters the woods, for a lesser rockier track on the left.

Descend by a wall, then go right, through the wall and soon, past a large beech, drop to a lower bracken-clad terrace with a 4-way signpost. Continue straight ahead along the terrace which ends above the attractive cottages of Slack Head. A little further join the road whence a few minutes down left is sufficient to regain the start at Beetham.

Whilst in Beetham, have a look at the church which is one of the most attractive old buildings in the area. The original tower was Saxon, and there is some evidence of Norman work on the south side.

16. The Cross Sands Walk

Before the days of easy road and rail travel, Morecambe Bay was a notable short cut for travellers between Lancashire and Furness. The Roman Emperor Agricola may have used the crossing of the sands and it was certainly well used by the monks from the 7th century onwards. Soldiers, drovers and travellers regularly made the crossing.

Guides were established by the late 13th century to aid travellers in the dangerous crossing - for there were many cases of people vanishing into the quicksand. The tradition of a guide, appointed by the Duchy of Lancaster, is still upheld, with the present incumbent guide, Cedric Robinson.

The crossing is usually made by large guided parties in summer when the tides are favourable. In June 1985, the old tradition of horse-drawn carriages crossing the sands was revived by a group which included the Duke of Edinburgh - again guided by Cedric Robinson.

Whilst the crossing appears innocent enough, especially when successfully accomplished on one of the guided walks, dangers abound with areas of quicksand and the chance of being overtaken by the incoming tide - which floods the shallow basin so quickly that it could not be outrun by man or horse. If you have seen the incoming bore race up the estuary to Arnside you will realise the implications. Channels in the sand vary, especially after a rough winter. Since 1985 the crossing is only feasible from Silverdale or Arnside to Grange, due to the dangers of crossing the Keer Channel on the longer route from Hest Bank. The guide knows just where the passage is safe and **the walk must only be done on one of the organised crossings.**

The traditional long crossing was from Hest Bank to Kent's Bank, between 8 to 12 miles according to route. Shorter routes linked Silverdale to Grange or Kent's Bank. There is a four-hour period, two hours either side of low water when the crossing is safe.

The first hazard from Hest Bank was the crossing of the Keer Channel, a notorious area of quicksands, then the route kept along sandbanks almost parallel to the coast until opposite Silverdale, where the route swung across the Kent Channel to another sandbank which leads to Kent's Bank. Recently the Kent Channel has swung much nearer to the Silverdale shore, and it is only feasible to make the crossing from Silverdale, although it could quite easily change again.

Guided crossings are huge, jolly affairs which attract many youngsters. Rarely is the party less than 100, often much more. The party assembles at an arranged spot, perhaps Jenny Brown's Point or even Arnside and the guide eventually appears, complete with large poking stick. He sets off like the Pied Piper of Hamelin followed by a capering crowd of children anxious to be in the vanguard. Behind trundles the main bulbous crowd, those in its centre seeing little but the feet and bodies of everyone around. Dress is usually T-shirt and shorts, or trunks. Footwear; plimsolls, trainers or nothing. Behind the main crowd are small groups of more thoughtful walkers who are trying to savour the broad expanse of a crossing and ignore the bustling crowd upfront.

The guide stops at a potential hazard, waits for the stragglers to catch up, waves his stick for silence and asks everyone to spread out for the crossing of a channel which if proddled by too many feet in one place could turn into quicksand. Children seem oblivious of the dangers, jump up and down in groups to set up a see-saw effect on the sand - which soon resembles a shaking jelly. With an imperious wave of the stick the guide sets forth again and the party resumes its course.

The Kent Channel requires a long wade of varying depth from knee to waist-deep. Dogs splash through and unconcernedly splash their fellow travellers. In the middle of the sands the shore looks far away and it is time to reflect on the dangers of the racing incoming tide - if you didn't know that you were in safe hands. Scramble out of the channel onto a long spit of firm sand that leads straight to the station at Kent's Bank, where you can buy a certificate stating that you have successfully made the crossing. People depart by coach, car or wait for the next train back to Silverdale.

On a nice, clear, sunny day the way is pleasant, some would say boring - with wide horizons and no difficulties. Poor visibility brings an eerie quality.

Do not be tempted to make the crossing unguided for the timing and route is critical. Dates and times of the crossings are advertised in the local press - *The Lancaster Guardian,* and *The Morecambe Visitor*. The first crossings of the year are usually in early June.

17. Linear Walks

Several excellent linear walks spring readily to mind, based on starting and finishing at railway stations or a main road. The following are merely suggestions.

Carnforth to Arnside

From the station turn left on the main road towards Warton until just over the River Keer turn right along a lane and meadows to Warton. Follow Walk No.4, over Warton Crag to the green lane, turn left down this to Crag Foot. Two hundred yards along the Silverdale road turn left by the dyke, go under the railway, cross a bridge right to gain the embankment. Follow this across the marsh, climb steeply over Heald Brow (Walk No.3 in reverse) to Woodwell and Silverdale village. Either go by the coast or Eaves Wood and Arnside Tower, over Arnside Knott, or round it, to the station.

The coast can be followed all the way if the tide allows. Start on a lane on the southern side of the River Keer at Carnforth, cross it at a bridge and continue to Cote Stones Farm on the edge of the salt marsh. A track leads towards Ings Point to join another track from Brown's Houses under Heald Brow. Make sure it is not a period of high tides before crossing the marsh.

Other routes can be made around the eastern base of Warton Crag, on the Coach Road for a short way to join Walk No.3 above Yealand Conyers. Continue on Walk No.4 in reverse over Cringlebarrow and Yealand Hall Allotment, cross Gait Barrows to Hawes Water. Join Walk No.7 to Hazelslack, finish over Arnside Moss.

Carnforth to Milnthorpe

The latter suggestion could be extended over Fairy Steps and Dallam Park (Walk No.14) to Milnthorpe.

Top: Arnside Tower
Below: Arnside

Farleton Fell
and
Hutton Roof

The spiny summit of Farleton Fell

Two small hills of exceptional interest lie apart from the main Silverdale-Arnside area. These hills lie a few miles to the east, across the flat low basin which carries the Lancaster-Kendal road, the canal, the motorway and a host of tiny lanes. A familiar sight to travellers is Farleton Fell, with a distinctive terraced hillside rising to the top of a grey scree cone which almost overshadows the motorway. Hutton Roof Fell is less obvious - a gently rising wooded slope crowned by

White Creek with Humphrey Head across the bay. Walks 2 & 11

an extensive limestone pavement. On its eastern side, above the attractive little village of Hutton Roof, are the sloping tile-like crags from which it derives its name.

The fell tops provide the main interest - large areas of bare limestone. On Farleton Fell the pavements are open and prospects wide, from Morecambe Bay to the Lakeland hills on one hand, the Pennines on the other. On Hutton Roof, the reverse applies, for the limestone is like a giant maze. Prickly bushes which sprout from the many crevices abound and progress off the paths is akin to exploration. The limestone is massive and the tracks cut between head-high rocks. If unsure of your whereabouts, scramble to a high rock and scan the horizon like a mariner searching for sight of land, but here it is a sea of rock. Paths skirt the rock maze but for an afternoon's adventure a probe into the interior is great fun. There is nothing quite like it anywhere else in Britain.

Only one right of way footpath crosses the area, from Holme Park to Hutton Roof village, but outside the farmland and protected nature reserves there seems to be no objection to walking the tops. In recent years Farleton Fell has regrettably become a popular venue for motor bike scrambling.

The area is renowned amongst naturalists for its exceptionally interesting flora, protected in two extensive reserves. In late spring/ early summer the early purple orchid is prolific. The sheltered limestone crevices, or grykes, provide a perfect habitat for a range of interesting plants, some of which you would expect to see on a woodland floor. Often, you will see flowers here when they are long past their best in more open surroundings. Particular plants to look for in the grykes are the many species of fern - hart's tongue, hard shield and male; the wall and maidenhair spleenwort, the limestone polybody. The pavement is also an ideal habitat for herb robert, dog's mercury, dog violet and a host of other plants. Needless to say, these plants are protected by the Wildlife and Countryside Act, which makes it an offence to pick any wild flower without the owner's permission.

There is evidence of ancient settlements in the Hutton Roof area, at Grass Slacks to the north-east of the village. Some of the place names are fascinating - Uberash Plain, the Blasterfoot Gap and Ploverlands. At the edge of the woods on the south-west flank of Hutton Roof Fell is the tiny hamlet of Dalton. Dalton Old Hall, now a farm, was built in the Elizabethan style in 1666. Nearby are the remains of an old village which was depopulated by the plague. At that time Dalton was in the parish of Warton, but Warton refused to bury the plague victims. Burton took compassion and Dalton joined Burton.

Burton, the largest village in the area was once an important staging post between Lancaster and Kendal.

The following two walks, starting from the lane which rises between the two fells can be combined to give a very enjoyable day, but don't leave Hutton Roof too late, or you may find yourself lost in the maze!

18. Farleton Fell Just over 800ft. (No spot height on O.S. maps)
3¹/₂ miles
2 hours

Start from the lane between Farleton Fell and Hutton Roof Fell. The lane leaves the A6070 about half a mile north of Burton, just before Clawthorpe Hall. Turn right and drive uphill not quite to the highest point, where there is a lay-by on the right, facing the start of a gated track.

Follow the track and soon fork right past scratchings amongst the stones, to bear left as the track mounts the first scar. The main track bears right soon after, but we keep straight on, up the next short scar onto the bare bones of the flat fell. There is a slight track just to the right of a wall, which keeps mainly to the ribbon of grass between the rocks, although bare clints have to be crossed in places. The scene is one of chaotic desolation, with grey rocks everywhere. Stunted hawthorns, like black scarecrows, poke out of crevices. A green valley comes in from the right - drop down a slight slope at the head of this and turn left over a stile to follow another wall towards a fine array of rock slabs ahead. There is a perched rock table on the right, a relic of glaciation, and a most attractive rocky hollow. The limestone clints are massive here, with old yews and hawthorns guarding the maze of rock. It is almost like a petrified glacier, a tumble of grey, water-worn limestone blocks. The rundkarren grooves - water channels are especially good and create a fine natural sculpture.

The way goes up a grass channel between the wall and sea of tilted limestone slabs. Just below the crest of the rise cross a stile on the left which gives access to the summit of the fell on the left. It is a fine top, on a house ridge of bare rock, perched on the edge of a tiered crag.

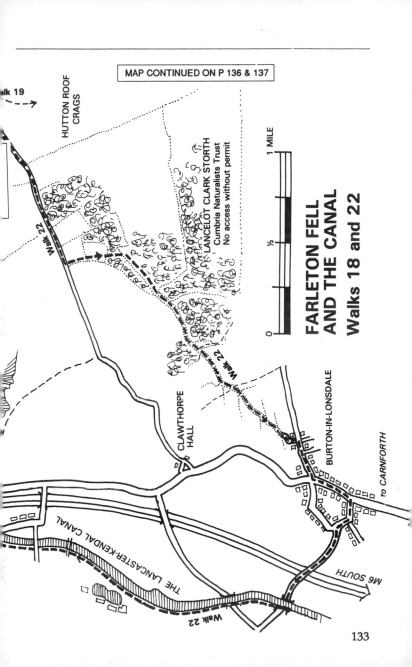

MAP CONTINUED ON P 136 & 137

Walk 19

HUTTON ROOF CRAGS

Walk 22

LANCELOT CLARK STORTH
Cumbria Naturalists Trust
No access without permit

Walk 22

1 MILE

½

0

**FARLETON FELL
AND THE CANAL
Walks 18 and 22**

CLAWTHORPE HALL

BURTON-IN-LONSDALE

to CARNFORTH

THE LANCASTER-KENDAL CANAL

M6 SOUTH

Walk 22

Walk 22

133

On Farleton Fell

As befits such a commanding position, the views are exceptionally good all round, from the Lakeland fells and the Pennines on one hand and the Silverdale hills and Morecambe Bay on the other.

Return to cross the stile, turn left and continue by the wall side. The track soon drops sharply and there are good views left of the crags, which lie below the summit. We are heading for cairns on the lower summit, really a plateau which overlooks the steep north-western nose of the fell. There are several cairns and the busy M6 buzzes directly below. Return on the grassy spine of the plateau, past two more cairns and the odd erratic boulder of sandstone, transported here on ice by long gone glaciers.

We can regain our outward path or make a variation return along the descending shelf we are on, which gives a change of scene above the pastoral shallow valley of Lupton Beck. There is a good path on the shelf. Cross a wall and continue through a patch of gorse to a tractor track. This descends, so take a small path on the continuation of the shelf to join a better path as the shelf swings gradually round. Keep on the top side of a walled enclosure and soon meet the top of the tarmac lane. Turn down this to the lay-by and your car, or continue along a signed path straight ahead towards Hutton Roof Crags which is described as the next walk.

Rock table on Farleton Fell

19. Hutton Roof Crags from the lane between Farleton Fell and Hutton Roof Fell

Mileage is small and time is as long as you care to make it!

Hutton Roof Crags deserve more than a single visit; indeed it takes several visits to comprehend the complex terrain. There are so many variations possible in this compact area that it is difficult to recommend just one circuit. The following route takes one of the most obvious routes, other variations are suggested in the text and reference to the sketch map will enable the walker to plan alternative circuits. The immediate surroundings are so interesting that it is a good place to walk even on a day of limited visibility - but in mist it can be terribly confusing and is best avoided unless you want a navigational challenge with map and compass. Most of the paths traverse very rough and rocky ground, sometimes over bare limestone with many traps for the unwary. When the rock is bone-dry, there is no problem, but when wet the limestone is treacherously slippery. At such times great care is required and the Uberash Breast Spine route should be avoided.

There are two summits, at the north-east and south-west of a gently rising dome of limestone. The lower north-east summit is the most prominent and is the objective of this walk.

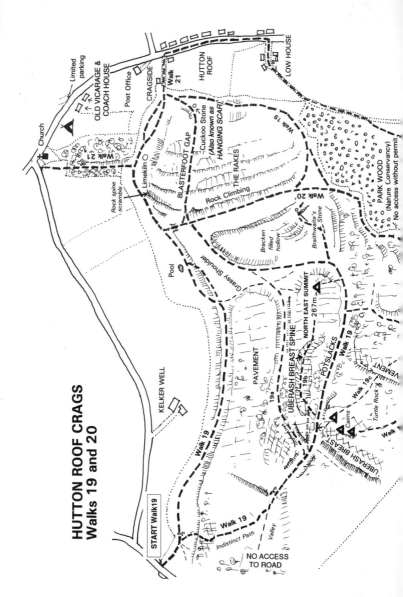

HUTTON ROOF CRAGS
Walks 19 and 20

Limited parking

Church

OLD VICARAGE & COACH HOUSE

Post Office

CRAGSIDE

Walk 21

HUTTON ROOF

LOW HOUSE

Walk 19

Walk 21

Limekiln

Cuckoo Stone
(Also known as
HANGING SCAR)

BLASTERFOOT GAP

THE RAKES

Rock Climbing

PARK WOOD
(Nature Conservancy)
No access without permit

Rock spine scramble

Walk 20

Braithwaite's Stone

Bracken filled hollow

Grassy Shoulder

Pool

KELKER WELL

PAVEMENT

NORTH EAST SUMMIT
267m

Walk 19

POTSLACKS

UBERASH BREAST SPINE

Walk 19a

Walk 19b

Walk 19c

PAVEMENT

Turtle Rock

Cairns

Walk

UBERASH BREAST

START Walk 19

Walk 19

Indistinct Path

Valley

NO ACCESS
TO ROAD

136

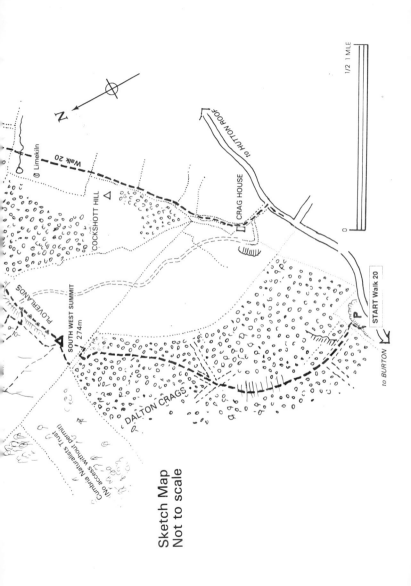

Sketch Map
Not to scale

N

1/2   1 MILE

to HUTTON ROOF

Walk 20

Limekiln

COCKSHOTT HILL

CRAG HOUSE

PLOVERLANDS

SOUTH WEST SUMMIT
274m

START Walk 20

P

to BURTON

DALTON CRAGS

Cumbria Naturalists Trust
(No access without permit)

137

Circuits are generally quite short, but distance and time bear no relation here. Allow an afternoon to explore the place, and note that the quickest return to the car from the eastern side is by the footpath which skirts the northern edge of the area.

Start: There is ample parking on the verge close to the top of the lane which separates Farleton Fell from Hutton Roof. This lane branches from the main road about ¹/₂ mile north of Burton, signed 'Clawthorpe.'

A stile at the highest point of the lane gives access to the fell on the right. Follow the path for 100 yards until opposite where the wall on the left bends away. Here take a small track which forks right, then bends to mount a slight scar on the right. Cross a short stretch of bare rock after which the track is indistinct, but head towards a little valley where a more definite path is joined. Turn left, up the valley and pass a little defile defended by gorse. Just past a bracken-filled hollow the path splits, take the right path (left is 19a) which mounts by the left end of a long line of crags - Uberash Breast. At the highest point of the path it is worth making a short diversion onto the limestone pavement on the right, where there are three cairns, a good viewpoint to get bearings. Our route can be seen, following a slight valley with the rocky cone of the N.E. summit on its left. On the far side of the summit lies a parallel narrower defile which carries the path of 19a. Between the two defiles is a long, swelling rib of bare rock, the Uberash Breast Spine, which forms the adventurous scramble of 19b. The three cairns overlook a fine pavement on the edge of a rising plateau - 19c describes a loop to the S.W. summit.

Return to the high point of the path in the defile and follow this through several undulating hollows, named Potslacks on the O.S. map. Emerge from the trees where tilted slabs on the left rise to the N.E. summit (267m 897ft.). It is best to pass the slabs before mounting to the top. The near view is predominantly rocky, although stubby prickly bushes sprout everywhere. The S.W. summit can be seen, and ahead are the crags of The Rakes with the long line of the Pennines across the Lune Valley. Ingleborough's flat top is easily distinguished, as is the deep trench of Barbondale further left. The smooth Howgill Fells to the north link the Pennines to the eastern fells of the Lake District.

From the summit regain the path and follow it left below the rocks. There are several returns from here - either by 19a, a path which runs in a narrow rocky defile parallel to the one we have followed, or go further on the grassy shoulder to join the major path which runs from Hutton Roof village along the northern edge of the crags. This follows a shelf and affords the easiest route.

However, there is much of interest on the eastern side of the fell, before returning. Between the summit and the long crag of The Rakes is a large bracken-filled hollow. A slight track down grass leads into the hollow and at its narrow right-hand (south) end is a large squat boulder. This bears a well carved inscription, 'John Braithwaite, Blacksmith 1836,' complete with carved horseshoe. Graffiti - but so elegantly carved!

Climb out of the hollow and follow a path on its grassy rim to the bottom of the long line of crags. There is a gap between the crags and a wall, with a path through bracken. Descend and keep above a wall as the track swings below slabs of broken rock, pass a small quarry, with the houses of Hutton Roof village just across a field to the right. Another path is joined just below the Cuckoo Stone; a prominent rock on a tiny plinth. Either go steeply up, past the Stone and through the Blasterfoot Gap, an interesting path which cuts the prominent roof tile-like slabs on the top of The Rakes, or go around the base of the hill, with the wall on the right. A path comes in from the village, turn left up velvet-like grassy paths, past a limekiln on the left (see Walk No.21). Just past the limekiln is the steep start of a rocky ridge, which affords an exciting scramble for those who like rock.

The path rises gently, past the track on the left from the Blasterfoot Gap, to a small pool. Here, rise on to the next shelf and continue pleasantly below the limestone pavement back to the car.

The early purple orchid

Variants

19a. This is an interesting, confined path in a narrow rocky defile.

19b. Uberash Breast Spine - a long hump of bare rock which has been likened to a basking whale. Surrounded by dense bushes, the best route is along the crest of the bare spine. Access is best viewed from the three cairns, and is gained from the top of the main path. The spine descends gently towards the N.E. summit, which is gained over more broken rocks, or follow the rock spine right to join the path in Potslacks. Uberash Breast is the most exciting way to the summit, for anyone who likes rock scrambling, but must be avoided if at all damp, when it becomes unpleasant and dangerously slippery. If you enjoy this, note that there is another spiny scramble, starting near the old limekiln just above Hutton Roof village, but this has a steep start on big holds, before easing into a rocky walk.

19c. S.W. Summit from the Three Cairns
The cairns stand on the edge of a bare plateau, at the far end of which lies the highest point of Hutton Roof Crags. This can be incorporated

GREAT COUM   GRAGARETH

into the walk by the following little circuit. From the cairns head diagonally across the plateau to join a little track which heads towards a low tree-topped scar. Just before the scar note the unusual Turtle Rock on the right. The track continues in the same line, past a dip to join the grassy slopes of Ploverlands. A cairned rise leads to the trig. point at the S.W. summit.

The return to the Three Cairns can be made directly - pass to the left of another cairn on a limestone pavement, and follow a slight track which becomes indistinct near to the Three Cairns.

20. A circuit of Hutton Roof Crags from Plain Quarry
4½ miles
3 hours

A pleasant circuit of the south-eastern part of the fell, which includes a good mix of woodland and open fell walking.

Uberash Breast Spine

INGLEBOROUGH
NE SUMMIT, HUTTON ROOF CRAGS

The three Cairns. Hutton Roof Crags

Start: Plain Quarry is a large gravel-filled quarry which lies 2 miles from Burton on the Whittington road, which leaves the A6070 at the south end of the village.

Near the middle of the quarry car park, take a small path which rises on the quarry edge. In 50 yards bear left into the woods. The path soon joins another which comes in from the left and rises steadily on a rocky shelf, with pleasant views across the Silverdale hills and the bay. The trees are quite small and the path quieter than its counterparts around Silverdale. Enter a thicket and reach another track. Turn right along this and fork left almost immediately. It develops into a tunnel-like avenue between the trees. Continue past a clearing on the left (views) where the path swings right to the edge of the wood and a stile in a fence onto the open fell. Go 30 yards right to a through stile in the wall. (Note: A stile at the left corner of the wall no longer exists.)

The next field to the left is protected by the Cumbrian Trust for Nature Conservation. Access is only allowed with special permission from the Trust at Church Street, Ambleside. It is of special interest to botanists for its limestone flora.

The S.W. summit of Hutton Roof Crags (274m) lies about 100 yards across the open fell and its trig. point forms a fine viewpoint of the Pennines, with Ingleborough's dark prow prominent. Just beyond the summit the grassy area is named Ploverlands, and with any luck you should see plovers here. Go north-east along a cairned grass crest to its end where it drops towards the tangle of limestone pavement and scrub. We have two choices, both interesting. The easiest route is to follow Option 1.

Option 1

From the end of the grass crest bear right to a wall which bounds the top edge of dense woods. Here you will find a tenuous track which

South west summit, Hutton Roof Crags

twists an intricate course between clints and prickly bushes. The track leaves the wall to enter a small valley but then regains the wall side which it follows closely below confined crags as it descends. Near the end of the wood rise through a little gap in the crags and you will see ahead a line of several parallel crags - The Rakes - the uppermost of which is almost unbroken and a popular practice ground for rock climbers. We have more alternatives here - one path descends to the right by the wall and rounds the southern edge of The Rakes before it swings north above a wall to join the recommended route at the Cuckoo Stone.

The most interesting way goes up the grassy sward below the long line of the climbing crag straight ahead. At its head is a little col and a major path junction just beyond. Turn right and go through a rocky gap to see the path dropping through more rocky gaps as it descends through The Rakes. This is the Blasterfoot Gap, an interestingly rocky area. On either hand are seas of limestone slabs, like a series of breaking waves, some of the most attractive in the area and justly famed for karren grooves - rounded water-eroded channels in the surface of the sloping limestone, which form a beautiful sculpted pattern. Who needs the Tate Gallery when nature provides such wonderful art?

The long straggle of Hutton Roof village lies directly below, as our path descends very steeply past a curious boulder - the Cuckoo Stone - balanced precariously on a small base and crowned by tiny bushes. Swing left above the wall then right to a gate and short lane which joins the village road.

The Cuckoo Stone

Option 2

From the end of the grass crest after Hutton Roof summit, this route takes as direct a line as possible to the N.E. summit (267m) - its cairn visible across a slight intervening valley. It is not far but the terrain is tortuous amongst a maze of limestone clints defended by lines of prickly bushes. You stray from the tiny tracks at your peril! Description of the route is difficult and it is really a test of navigational skills as you sometimes seem to be going in circles as the path twists to avoid particularly dense patches of bush. However, with the aid of the sketch map and the following comments I will send you on your way in the hope that once in the maze you will be able to get out!

From the end of the cairned grass crest, take a small sheep track left, drop over a little rock shelf where a track leads right in the dip. Where the crag bends right, bear left over a limestone pavement and down a gap in the bushes into a sheltered hollow. This is the little valley which runs through the clints. Turn left a few yards, then fork right round the top side of a line of crags. The track is going more or less in the direction we need and pops out at another N.W.-S.E. hollow which runs through the clints. Here turn right along a path which runs below an area of rock slabs, at the far end of which go left to the cairned summit. Dead easy if you got it right first time! Return to the path which swings round the rocky end of the clints and emerge onto open grass slopes.

Ahead is the long diagonal climbing crag at the head of The Rakes. Our path keeps left above a line of crags and joins Option 1 at the little col at the head of the crags, where keep straight on down the Blasterfoot Gap to the village.

Turn right and walk the quiet village lane, pleasant enough with its flower-decked walls and stone cottages. About half-way, on the wall of a low building is a circular, yellow enamelled AA sign, a rarity these days. It states the name of the village and distances to nearby towns - and London 252¼ miles.

At the end of the village a path signed 'Crag House' goes right through the junk-yard of Low House. Once past the rusting paraphernalia of farm machinery the lane becomes very pleasant as it enters the National Nature Reserve of Park Wood. A notice at the entrance informs us that the reserve was bought by the Nature Conservancy in 1979 and is an interesting example of woodland on limestone. The lower part of the wood, which is visible from our path, lies on deeper soils than the upper and contains much coppiced wych elm, ash and a rich, varied ground flora. The sparse soil of the upper wood is covered by dense hazel scrub and coppiced ash, with occasional field maple here near to its northern limit in Britain. Permits to visit the wood can be obtained from the Reserve Warden, Orchard Cottage, Waterslack, Silverdale, Carnforth, LA5 0UH. Our path skims the bottom edge of the wood. It is interesting to note that we are walking almost on top of the Thirlmere Aqueduct at this point.

Go along the lane to the second reserve notice where a path enters the field below the wood, which makes a pretty sight especially in bluebell time. There are several springs along the base of the limestone which here rests on impervious gritstones. Over a stile, cross a tiny stream which issues from a strong spring just above, and go below a ruined limekiln, along a broad smooth shelf. Keep on this shelf left of the little pimple of Cockshott Hill, at the top edge of the meadow, to join a rough lane which leads through the farmyard of Crag House to the road. Turn right and a few minutes walk leads back to Plain Quarry and the car.

The Turtle Rock
(See Walk 19c p. 140)

Hutton Roof Church

21. Hutton Roof Crags from the village

Much of the best walking on Hutton Roof is described on the preceding walks, but a start from Hutton Roof village can be equally convenient. At the northern end of the village, just before the church, is Cragside, an attractive campsite.

There are two access paths from the village - one by a short lane just south of the post office, the other from the lane at the side of the church. A glance at the accompanying map will show the combinations possible. Note the old limekiln which is close to the junction of the two paths. The bowl where the lime was burnt can be seen lined with hard baked sandstone.

Parking in the village is difficult. There is space for a few cars about half-way between the village and the church.

The Canal

The Preston to Lancaster canal was built at the height of the canal boom - construction work began on the Kendal to Lancaster section in 1796 and the section was opened in 1819. Coal was transported from the Lancashire coal-fields to feed industry in Kendal and the coconut matting factory at Holme; whilst the produce of the Kendal area was transported to the markets of Lancashire. However, the prosperity was short-lived as railways and better roads made canals a poor alternative. It was closed to commercial traffic in 1947 and closed to navigation by the Transport Act of 1955. The building of the M6 finalised the possibility of navigation for it cut the canal permanently. Now the canal is culverted under several roads and completely blocked by the motorway north of Holme.

Lack of traffic on the stretch north of Tewitfield has proved its worth, for the canal is a place of true tranquillity. Wildlife is prolific and the water has taken on a clarity lacking on other sections. Moorhen and coot nest in the sedge, pike can be glimpsed in the water. Mallard and swans share the water with heron. A walk on the tow-path - a pleasant dry trod of close-cropped turf, is almost certain to be rewarded by the sight of 10 to 20 species of birds. The Lancaster Canal Trust is advocating a linear park north of Tewitfield with marinas, restaurant, boating and a host of other tourist activities. It would be disastrous if such a development were allowed to take place. One only has to walk the section used by powered craft south of Tewitfield to see the difference in quality.

A feature of the canal is the typical little stone bridge with a beautiful elliptical arch, designed by John Rennie. Conifers around the bridge approaches add to their charm.

Despite the proximity of the motorway, the traffic buzz is only distracting where the canal lies to windward. Long-distance ramblers traverse the whole length of the canal each year from Preston to Kendal. The following two walks are designed to suit the nature of this book - afternoon circuits of a gentle pace.

A recommended book which details the history of the canal is Robert Swain's *A Walkers Guide to the Lancaster Canal*, (Cicerone Press).

Hang-gliders over Farleton Fell, seen from the canal

22. A circuit from Holme - Farleton Fell, Burton, return along the canal

(See map p.133)
8¹/₂ miles
Approx. 3¹/₂ hours

The steep ascent of Farleton Fell is done early in the walk, whilst the return is a gentle stroll along the canal tow-path. Other starting points could be used just as well along the circuit.

Character: A bit of all sorts - a little lane walking, rough ground on Farleton Fell, and old drovers' lane and finally the greensward of the tow-path.

Start: There is space to park on a wide verge where the road which runs north from Holme curves to cut the canal and goes under the motorway to join the A6070.

Follow the tow-path north on the western bank of the canal which soon bends towards the motorway and ends abruptly against its embankment. Steps lead left, follow the edge of the field to a lane which crosses the motorway and the A6070 towards Farleton village. Leave the lane a few yards further at a bend where a sign points 'Footpath to Farleton Fell.'

Since the start, Farleton Fell has loomed prominently - a grey scree cone of impressive steepness. Our path goes straight up the field to a gate in the top left corner, which gives access to the open fell. There are slight tracks which take the direct challenge of the screes, but this is not recommended. Instead follow the path leftwards above a fringe of trees, but soon branch right along a steep incline - an old quarry path: this side of the fell has numerous tiny overgrown stone workings, too small to be called quarries, and traces of the old tracks can be seen in several places. (The lower track could also be taken although it loses height before following a parallel lower course.)

The incline ends at a working, but the rake continues with a narrow path, joins another track and gains height before traversing again through gorse. In places it is difficult to follow as it wiggles through the gorse jungle - a sea of vivid yellow in season and a good place to see linnet, birds with a reddish breast. Generally follow a traversing line leftwards and if you lose the path don't worry for it doesn't matter. In fact on a shelf, bear right then zig-zag up the open slopes, gradually leaving the gorse as height is gained. Numerous holes indicate that this is also rabbit country. If you keep slanting left you will encounter better paths. The fell top is elusive for each time you breast a rise another appears ahead until at last a small cairn appears - but another larger cairn lies just ahead, and at last this is the top - or one of the tops, for the true fell top lies the other side of a dip above a steep band of crags. Forget that for a while and enjoy the extensive panorama of the Lakeland fells and the Pennines.

The drone of the motorway is now a distant hum, but your peace may be shattered by the roar of two-stroke engines - this side of Farleton Fell is a favourite scrambling spot. The local Westmorland club organises several scramble events here, and despite the noise and rutted tracks, it provides great sport for youngsters. It is worth putting up with the noise for a while to see the skill and concentration as the young riders negotiate particularly awkward sections. As one adult rider said with a sweep of his hands 'You see all these hills around, yet there are few places we can go.

If you don't like the noise, press on and the rock hummocks soon deaden the sound.

Gain a path in the dip below the other rocky summit, and follow it over a rise. (Stile in the wall gives access to the summit.) Continue down with a fine area of rock slabs on the left, to a rocky hollow with limestone pavement. Keep by the wall, cross a stile at a fence and continue in the same line along a gentle dip. The path becomes more

Ingleborough is seen across the limestone clints

definite as it curves right. Below is a specially good platform of sculpted limestone, with Ingleborough behind. The track becomes a broad shelf as it swings right to reveal Morecambe Bay in the distance. It zig-zags left to cross a small rock scar and reaches the broad grass shelf with Hutton Roof Crags beyond.

Just before reaching the lane between the fells, note a stile over the wall to the right. This is a **short return** and goes across two fields to an old bridle track which runs along the edge of Holme Park Quarry to the A6070 at Holme Park. Turn left along the road and left at the first junction, under the M6 back to the car. The **longer return** now described is an easy walk and is recommended if time allows.

Turn right at the lane and follow it downhill for half a mile. It is quiet and attractively tree-lined. Go left at a sign 'Bridlepath to Burton Fell,' cross a field to enter woods through a gate, and turn right by a wall side through the next gate. This is an idyllic spot, with enough calm and peace to make the traffic and two-stroke noise seem another world. Few horses go this way for the path is hardly wide enough as it gently drops downhill. The path widens at the bottom entrance to the Cumbrian Trust for Nature Preservation Reserve, on the left. Purchase of the reserve was aided by the World Wildlife Fund. Access is by permit only from the Trust at Church Street, Ambleside. It is an outstanding habitat of limestone woodland and limestone pavement higher up the fell side.

The bridle track leaves the woodland but not the vegetation. It is walled by high hedges and in mid-summer the eager vegetation

Along the canal, Farleton Fell behind

encroaches so much that progress along the path is a matter of forcing through a rich flora with masses of white hedge parsley. This botanists' paradise continues to the first houses of Burton.

In pack-horse days, Burton was a staging post between Lancaster and Kendal, and a thriving market town with the most extensive corn market in the country. Decline started with the opening of the Lancaster-Kendal canal and now only the square and cross hint at its former importance.

Turn right to join the main road, then go left to the village centre, just before which turn right along the curiously named Neddy Hill. Pass Drovers Lane - a continuation of our bridle path and an indication that it was used by cattle drovers from Silverdale and Warton. Turn left along Station Lane, go under the canal bridge and gain access to the tow-path at the far side.

After this stint along lanes, it is pleasant to walk on grass again beside the tranquil canal. Mallard float lazily by, coot scuttle in and out of reeds, cattle come down to drink at the water's edge, peewits call from the bank - all very relaxing on the stroll back to the car. Pass the long straggling village of Holme, with its mill pond. During the 1800's the main employment here was the production of coconut matting. Look out for the old milestone along the canal side.

Tewitfield locks lie next to the M6

23. A circuit from Borwick - Capernwray, River Keer, Warton, Yealand Conyers, Tewitfield

8¹/4 miles
3¹/2 hours

This walk is less typical of the area than any other walk in the book, for only a short stretch is amongst woodland. There is much open meadow and some lane walking. Nevertheless, it has its charms and cannot be ignored. In early summer the banks of the canal are fringed with numerous flowers - wild geraniums, yellow and purple vetch, poppies and hedge parsley. The path along the banks of the Keer is the only riverside path in this book apart from the stretch by the River Kent on Walk No.24.

Start from the pleasant village of Borwick, which is reached by a road from the A6 just south of the A6070 Burton junction. Just before crossing the canal to the village, there is a rough lane right with room to park several cars.

Borwick Hall is a fine building, dominated by its original pele tower, probably built in the 13th or 14th century. Since then there have been many additions - the Whittington family built the north and east wings around 1550, but the Bindloss family was responsible for many of the later features. Robert Bindloss was a very well-known Kendal wool merchant who acquired the manor between 1567 and 1590. He built the great baronial hall and the west wing. The gatehouse, built around 1659 is a lovely building and the terraced gardens are very attractive. The Hall now belongs to the Lancashire Youth Clubs Association and is only occasionally open to the public, although much can be seen from a browse round the exterior, including a glimpse of the fine spinning gallery.

Gain the tow-path, and follow it south along the meandering canal. The banks are rich in wild geraniums and poppies. As Capernwray is approached, note the canal branch into the woods opposite. This is a mooring point and the woods hide a large caravan site. Just after the railway bridge the canal crosses the River Keer on an aqueduct at Keer Bridge. The river runs deep below, by the side of an attractive restored mill. Leave the canal at the next bridge and go along the tarmac lane for 50 yards to a fork. Go through a stile ahead into a field and diagonally right under a railway bridge to a footpath by the edge of the tiny River Keer. The stream runs between steep vegetated banks.

Cross a lane and continue on the opposite side of the river. A catwalk under the motorway leads to the edge of the large flooded gravel pits of Dock Acres. The path skirts the edge of these to the recently developed Pine Lake Resort. Pass the development by a gravel path close to the road, then a green path parallel to the busy A6.

Cross the A6 and go along a green lane, under a railway arch and between tall hedges. Emerge on a lane which goes into Warton village, turn left along the main street then right at the Black Bull up a steep rise to enter a car park at the foot of a small quarry. This is a popular rock climbing spot although in summer the crags are rather overgrown. There is a profusion of red valerian, escapees from nearby gardens.

The path goes up the floor of the quarry, richly wooded, through a wall and turns right at the junction with another path. Keep straight on at a junction, on a level path which skirts the top edge of meadow above the village. There are many paths in the woods, but keep just above the wall. Cross a wall and keep right at every junction, with the wall always on the right. Pass two bracken clearings, then continue in dense woods. Go left up past some prominent arrow marks to join the broad bridle track of Occupation Road. Turn down this to the tarmac lane, Coach Road.

Walk left along the lane for half a mile to a footpath on the right, signed 'Yealand Conyers.' Take this through a field, past an old limekiln and through patches of trees. Just before reaching a wall, fork left through an area of bushes with the wall on the right. This leads to a tarmac lane, down which turn right into the straggling village of Yealand Conyers. Turn left at the lane junction, then right along another lane soon after, which leads to the A6. Cross this and a farm lane opposite soon leads into fields. Keep to the wall side, descend towards the motorway, circle right and go under the motorway by a tunnel-like passage. On the far side gain the canal bank.

Follow the tow-path down the side of the once renowned Tewitfield locks, a staircase in the canal, now with no lock gates and transformed into a series of small waterfalls. Beyond the A6070 is the start of the navigable section of canal with the inevitable marina. After several bends and bridges we return to our starting point at Borwick.

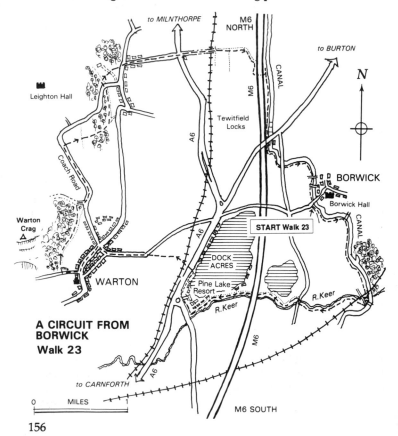

A CIRCUIT FROM BORWICK
Walk 23

24. Levens Park and Levens Hall
Allow about 2 hours for the walk, plus time spent at Levens Hall

This short but beautiful walk enhances a visit to Levens Hall, one of the most popular attractions of the area. The walk is described from the Sedgwick end of the Park. It is a walk completely different from others in this book, for it follows each side of the River Kent, the only major river in the area. Gentle where it flows through the Park, the more boisterous gorge at Sedgwick is not to be missed.

IMPORTANT The car park at Levens Hall is for visitors to the Hall only. Parking at the start of the walk must be <u>outside</u> the Park gates. Please keep to the right of way paths. Stray from them at your peril!

Start: The entrance to the park lies between Sedgwick and Hincaster on a minor lane. This can be reached most easily from the roundabout under the Kendal-M6 link road (A591). Follow the lane towards Sedgwick and over the River Kent turn right. The Park entrance is on the right just over the bridge crossing the M6 link.

The Park was laid out by Monsieur Beaumont between 1694 and 1710 and visitors are requested to treat this ancient park with respect and not leave litter or damage property. Notices at the entrance to the Park show the right of way path which must be strictly adhered to. Dogs must be on leads to avoid disturbance of the rare black fallow deer and the silken haired 'Bagot' goats - a breed peculiar to the park.

Follow the straight avenue of oaks which stretches away to the left for ³/₄ mile. This impressive landmark was under threat from the motorway link, but after vigorous protests the route was amended to avoid the Park. The right of way branches right (signed) to join the riverside and the A6, across which is the main driveway to Levens Hall.

Levens Hall dates from 1254 when a pele tower was built on the site of an earlier building. The park was enclosed around 1300. The present appearance of the house dates from Elizabethan times, when James Bellingham embarked upon a massive rebuilding programme, incorporating the pele tower into a magnificent building. Oak panelling, chimney pieces and carvings embellish the interior.

Levens Hall is renowned not only for its fine Elizabethan elegance, but for its unique topiary gardens which date from 1690. Visitors can still enjoy the weird shapes. There is also a garden centre and a collection of steam engines. The Hall and the gardens are only open to the public from Easter Saturday to the end of September, but the park is accessible all year.

To continue the walk return to the main road and cross the bridge. Almost immediately a signed footpath leads right into the park, soon rising up a grassy bank with the river in its wooded dell on the right. Keep on the path with the woods on the right and soon you are directed left at a 'Deer Sanctuary' sign. You may have seen the deer already, a herd of very unusual fallow deer, for their coats are dark brown.

The path crosses a wall to a field. Turn right and keep alongside the wall to reach a lane at Park Head cottages. Turn right along the lane which soon ends at the motorway link, but a catwalk leads under the wide bridge. Climbers use this as an all-weather training spot - note the chalk marks on the limestone cobbles, and the coloured paint blobs which guide the climber on traverses. Some authorities spend thousands of pounds on artificial climbing walls - this was purely accidental!

The lane continues again past Force Cottages, where the Kent falls over a limestone ledge to form a pretty waterfall. For several hundred yards the river flows in a deep gorge where vegetated limestone cliffs overhang ominous black pools. There are a few little tracks from the lane to the riverside, but these are fishermen's paths and lead nowhere - keep to the lane and be satisfied with glimpses into the gorge.

Above a wide pool is a fall with another fall close to a bridge. On the far bank there are many obvious remains of an old mill, with a wheel pit, a channel cut in the rock from the top fall to a tunnel, and various remains of buildings. This is the site of John Wakefield's Gunpowder Mill (1790). His first mill was built in 1764 just upstream, but moved to this site for a more powerful head of water. In 1850 production was moved again to Gatebeck on the River Bela where there was a 50-foot head of water. A horse-drawn tramway was built to join the railway at Milnthorpe in 1874. Kentdale was the gunpowder centre of the north - and also the centre of snuff-making at several mills nearer Kendal.

Turn right over the bridge - which forms a fine vantage point to study the river and the mill remains - and right again along a lane which leads back to the car.

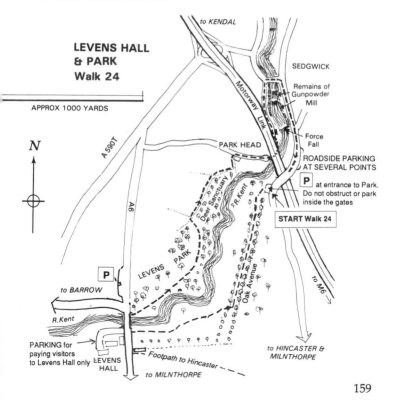

LEVENS HALL & PARK
Walk 24

APPROX 1000 YARDS

N

to KENDAL

SEDGWICK

Remains of Gunpowder Mill

Motorway Link

A 590 T

PARK HEAD

Force Fall

ROADSIDE PARKING AT SEVERAL POINTS

P at entrance to Park. Do not obstruct or park inside the gates

A6

Deer Sanctuary

R. Kent

START Walk 24

LEVENS PARK

Oak Avenue

to M6

P

to BARROW

R. Kent

PARKING for paying visitors to Levens Hall only

LEVENS HALL

Footpath to Hincaster

to HINCASTER & MILNTHORPE

to MILNTHORPE

Recommended further reading

The Wildlife of the Arnside-Silverdale Area. John Wilson and Peter Lennon, 1978. John Wilson is the RSPB Warden at Leighton Moss. Peter Lennon is a partner in Wildlife and Adventure Holidays. Essential background reading which covers the animal, bird and butterfly life of the area in detail.

In and Around Silverdale. David Peter, 1985. Local historian, David Peter has delved into the past to produce a fascinating book. Recommended to all visitors, although it only covers part of this guide area.

'Cross Kent Sands. David Peter, 1985. The history of crossing the sands of Morecambe Bay.

Sand Pilot of Morecambe Bay. Cedric Robinson - David and Charles, 1980.

One Man's Morecambe Bay. Cedric Robinson - Dalesman, 1984. The cross sands guide relates his experiences.

Warton: The Story of a North Lancashire Village. Morley, Smalley and Thornburrow, 1971.

Westmorland Heritage Walk. Mark Richards & Chris Wright - Cicerone Press 1987. A superb walk paying homage to the County of Westmorland.

In Search of Westmorland. Charlie Emett - Cicerone Press, 1985. A book full of anecdote and background history. Contains interesting details of the Kendal to Lancaster canal.

A Walker's Guide to the Lancaster Canal. Robert Swain - Cicerone Press, 1990. A complete guide to the Kendal-Preston canal.

Pettie Memories of a Victorian Nursery. Annie Beatrice Champion, (Edited and Illustrated by Avis Thornton). Excerpts taken from the notebooks of Annie Beatrice Champion recording her daily trials and joys as nanny of the Victorian nursery at Levens Hall.

The Chronicles of Milnthorpe. Roger Bingham - Cicerone Press
The history of a Cumbrian village.

Nature Trail Leaflets:

A Woodland Walk through Eaves Wood.
Warton Crag.
Arnside Knott: Three Walks.
The Beetham Trail.

Barrow Tide Tables available at Arnside or from Barrow Printing, Lawson Street, Barrow-in-Furness.

PRINTED BY
CARNMOR PRINT & DESIGN, LONDON ROAD, PRESTON